THIS THING called CHRISTIANITY

How To Get A Life That Makes A Difference

BRAD HUMPHREY

with
Teresa Vining

MOODY PRESS

CHICAGO

CONTENTS

The Spartans passed down to their young men a story they held up as an ideal.

It seems there was once a bright but undisciplined adolescent. He had caught a fox and was playing with it during a time reserved for study. Suddenly he looked up and saw his mentor coming down the road. There was no place to hide the fox, so he quickly stuffed the animal down his tunic and stood rigidly at attention.

In Spartan fashion, his instructor began asking him question after question about his lessons. Without raising his voice or making any sign of pain, the young man answered every question—even as the fox was literally tearing him apart inside.

Finally, in the midst of one answer, the youth fell dead at his teacher's feet—a shining example of Spartan courage.

Sadly, times haven't changed much.

Adolescence is a time when you most need to share your hurts and fears, questions and problems, goals and aspirations. Yet far too many teens hold it all inside— sometimes with disastrous results.

But there's hope. In fact, I feel strongly that your purchasing this workbook is a great step forward in discussing the most important area in your life—your relationship with Jesus Christ.

If you've been waiting for a tool that acts as a spiritual training and discussion guide, walking you through key growth areas, here's your source. It's written by my friend Brad Humphrey. He's a father and has been a "personal trainer" with young people for more than a decade, strengthening and encouraging their faith.

Brad speaks your language—not with hip talk and slang but through penetrating questions and exercises designed to help you see how "this thing called Christianity" applies to every area of life every day. From treating others with honor, to nailing down godly dating practices, to sharing plans and goals, to handling fear or lust, here's a tangible way to talk through crucial areas in your life.

Perhaps you're like me and come from a single-parent home. Or you don't have a godly example of a father and mother who talk through your tough issues. Whatever your situation, you've picked up a how-to manual designed to help you weave a fabric of faith into your life that can help you make a lifelong difference for Christ in your world.

JOHN TRENT, PH. D.

ACKNOWLEDGMENTS

God has blessed me with some incredible people throughout my life.

I want to thank my parents, Rusty and Pat Humphrey, who modeled for me what Christian love is. Dad, you were my first mentor.

I also want to thank my wife, Jeannie. God knew I needed a high "patient" in my life, who would accept me for who I am. Thanks for teaching me how to wait on people and for being my best friend.

Thanks also to Jeff Stokes. You are the business mate that God knew I would need to support this writing habit of mine. Thank you for being my Barnabas. To Teresa Vining, thanks for helping with my writing efforts. I also want to thank Jeff, Jeremiah, Shawn, Jimmy, Steve, Mike, Jon, and Mikey W., the "guinea pigs" for Promise Makers. You guys turned my efforts into a life-changing experience. Each of you is a model of a true Promise Maker. I wish I'd had friends like you when I was in high school.

Finally, I want to thank my God. Lord, You are so wonderful, and You have richly blessed this earthly life of mine. I pray that You will take pleasure in what this book represents and will bless all those young people who make a study of its contents. And may Your eyes continue to move "to and fro throughout the earth," finding young believers who will promise to give their hearts completely to You. You deserve nothing less!

NOTE FROM THE AUTHOR

As I have talked with, observed, counseled, and mentored believers over the past fifteen years, I have noticed several problem areas that keep good people from living their lives for Christ. It is these critical problem areas that I am attempting to address in this book. I strongly believe that each of these areas is critical to your long-term success as a Christian living in a world hungry to claim you as its next victim.

My prayer is that you will personalize every area discussed in this book. I am convinced that if you dedicate yourself to seeking and living God's truth, He will bless your life with abundant wisdom and grace. Commit yourself to spending the time necessary to allow God to reveal to you some of His wonderful treasures. Listen closely to the leader of your Promise Makers* group as he (or she)

*Promise Makers was the original name given to a Bible study for high school men that Brad led in his home. It is not affiliated in any way with the Promise Keepers Ministry. Since this first group, small groups of high school age men and women have begun meeting. Their focus is to grow in their accountability to Jesus Christ, and they have used the materials contained in this book to assist in this effort. Brad is co-founder of Accountable Christian Living, a ministry that helps Christians of all ages become more accountable in their walk with God, with other Christians, and in their school or jobs.

tries to relate what he has learned. Think of him as your mentor and do not be quick to judge him. God is still working in your leader's life also.

I have struggled with every area discussed in this book. I had trouble understanding who I was in Christ. I didn't always date in a manner that glorified God, and I have certainly had times when spending time with Him was not my highest priority. I praise God for my parents, who prayed consistently for me while I was struggling through all these things in high school. But even with supportive parents, I still had difficulty making it through the teens.

Your teen years are some of the most important years of your life. What you do with these years will greatly determine who you will be during adulthood. Many think that they can wait until they are adults to get serious about serving God. But by the time they are adults, they have already messed up their lives with bad decisions and habits, making it difficult to come back to God. In addition, they have wasted several years in which they could have been growing spiritually.

I am convinced that, regardless of your family background, if you determine to live for Christ, you can succeed in all areas of life through His love and power. He knows your needs, and He knows how to meet those needs. He is always faithful. Many times He provides us with more provisions than we could ever dream of.

Make your first promise today. Promise to open up your life to God over these next few months of study. Allow your leader and the other Promise Makers in your group to hold you accountable for implementing God's truth in your life.

Use this book as a resource. Write notes in it. Record

your fears and dreams in it. After you have completed it, go back through it again for insights that you may have missed. Refer to it as you face obstacles over the next few years.

And keep in mind that becoming a Promise Maker is serious business. Many Christians make promises, but the ones who stand out above the crowd are those who keep the promises they make.

I can't wait to see you in heaven and hear about all the things God chose to do in your life. May God bless you, and may you always make promises that glorify Him.

See you inside the Pearly Gates!

BRAD HUMPHREY

BECOMING A PROMISE MAKER

Welcome to Promise Makers.

Your Promise Makers group is not a club or civic organization but, rather, a fellowship of young Christians who share the number one goal of becoming who God wants them to be.

Becoming a Promise Maker involves examining crucial areas of your life and making important promises about those areas, promises that you are seriously committed to keeping.

The goal is not to give you a new list of rules but, rather, to help you realize the significance of going God's way in all spheres of life.

In the next several weeks, we will explore eight topics that represent critical areas in the lives of most young people. At the end of each study, you will be given the opportunity to make a promise to God to obey Him in that area.

Although your promises will be made only to Him, you will have the privilege of talking about them with other Christians. Proverbs 27:17 says, "Iron sharpens iron, so one man sharpens another." In other words, other believers can make us "sharper" in our efforts to love and serve Christ.

It is critical that we learn how to talk openly with other believers and how to love and support each other. Most men, for example, as they grow older, tend to shy away from being honest with other men.

Remember, the things you do now and the decisions you make now are determining the person you will become. So *now* is the time to make commitments to God, *before* you become entangled with the effects of bad choices. Nailing down issues now will help prepare you for the challenges you will face later on and will help you become the person God wants you to be.

There is no limit to what He can do through you when you give every aspect of your life to Him.

For the eyes of the Lord move to and fro throughout the earth that He may strongly support those whose heart is completely His.
2 Chronicles 16:9

We live in a crucial time. We are surrounded by news of murder, violence, scandal, the weakening of the family, and the decline of moral values. God is looking for "a few good men"—and women—whom He can use to change the course of the future, men and women who will be instrumental in leading others to Him, men and women who will help turn back the tide of evil that is sweeping across the nation.

You may not hear it on the evening news, but God is already doing some amazing things in this world. He is using young men and women just like you to bring unprecedented numbers of people to Himself. He is using men and women just like you to influence the neighborhoods of America, and He is using men and women just like you to help rebuild the moral values of this country.

The opportunities and challenges that face us are great. How then do we prepare ourselves to make a difference for Christ? How do we keep ourselves from falling into the same traps that others before us have fallen into—impurity, materialism, dishonesty, egotism, devastating indebtedness? And how do we equip ourselves for our mission?

The place to start is by making decisions *now* regarding critical areas of our lives, commitments that we intend to keep. Promises.

PROMISE MAKING

The Bible often calls it a "vow." Some call it "giving their word." In both situations an individual is making a promise. A promise involves pledging to do something—or not to do something. And in making a promise, one commits to being accountable to whomever the promise is made.

Promises are serious business with God. Numbers 30:2 says, "If a man makes a vow to the Lord, or takes an oath to bind himself with a binding obligation, he shall not violate his word; he shall do according to all that proceeds out of his mouth."

In Ecclesiastes 5:4–5, we find an even stronger emphasis on how important it is to God that we keep our promises: "When you make a vow to God, do not be late in paying it. . . . Pay what you vow! It is better that you should not vow than that you should vow and not pay."

That's pretty intimidating, but for Christians there is good news. Paul says in Philippians 4:13, "I can do all things through Him who strengthens me."

Since Christ is in us—as a result of our accepting the gift of His sacrifice for our sins—His strength is available to help us fulfill the commitments we make. Jesus died so that we could have a relationship with Him and also be victorious in this life.

Following Christ is not just a requirement for those Christians who plan to be missionaries or pastors. It is Christ's expectation for all believers. Romans 12:1 says, "I urge you therefore, brethren, by the mercies of God, to present your bodies a living and holy sacrifice, acceptable to God, which is your spiritual service of worship."

Christ loves us unconditionally. However, when we accept Him as Savior, He calls us to a life of service and obedience, and it is our responsibility to commit ourselves to this calling. Promises are not to be entered into lightly, but making commitments to God about how we will act and think is the beginning of fulfilling this responsibility—of becoming the men and women God wants us to be.

Make vows to the Lord your God and fulfill them.
Psalm 76:11

Weekly Commitments of a Promise Maker

The world's finest athletes realize their dreams and goals only through the practice of a vast array of disciplines. Through proper diet, they take in those foods that contribute to optimum energy level and muscle reformation. Through specialized conditioning, they tone and strengthen their bodies. Through intense mental rehearsal, they develop their strategy for winning.

Growing as a Christian also requires nourishment, conditioning, and strategic planning.

Our nourishment is supplied through the reading of

God's Word, which provides the proper nutrition to transform our thinking and behavior.

Our conditioning comes through putting into practice the directives and guidelines that we gain from Bible study.

And our strategic planning comes through meeting with others, where we discuss our problems and concerns. It is through these "strategy sessions" that we can review our failures and put new game plans in place.

Each Promise Makers session will consist of the following:

- Review of the past week's successes and failures
- Discussion of God's Word regarding the session's topic
- Discussion of the application of the material to our lives
- Disclosing the promises we have made
- Prayer time for God's leadership in each of our lives

In addition to attending each Promise Makers session and making sure the appropriate section of the workbook is completed beforehand, each Promise Maker will be involved in the following disciplines:

- Verse memorization (1–2 per week)
- Daily quiet time (10 minutes minimum)
- Promise Makers journal (3 entries minimum per week)
- Church attendance (taking notes at a minimum of one sermon or Bible study class per week)

Being successful in Christian living is possible but only as we surrender every part of our lives to Christ. Following the regimen laid out above can help instill the disciplines necessary to follow Jesus and become a man or woman of God who never will have to be ashamed.

In Thee, O Lord, I have taken refuge; let me never be ashamed.
Psalm 71:1

Promise 1

THIS THING CALLED CHRISTIANITY

Christy had been going to church with her parents since before she could remember, and she considered herself a pretty good Christian. She knew all the basic Bible stories, and she even volunteered to help in the nursery at church every once in a while. She tried to be a good person, and she usually treated people in the way she would want to be treated. Then she started dating Ryan.

There was something different about Ryan. Ryan seemed to have a genuine relationship with God, and he seemed so sure of what he believed and so committed to it. On their first date, Ryan had asked Christy if she was a Christian, and, of course, she had said she was. But after hanging around Ryan, she began to wonder. She knew she believed in God and in the Bible. But was there something she was missing? The more she got to know Ryan, the more she realized that her kind of Christianity and his kind were not the same. But what was the difference? And was it possible for her to have the certainty that Ryan had about his relationship with God?

WILL THE REAL CHRISTIANS STEP FORWARD, PLEASE?

Many people call themselves Christians. Especially in America, you can ask almost anyone and you will receive answers such as, "Sure, I'm a Christian. I was raised in church," or, "Sure, I'm a Christian. I believe in God and am basically a good person."

The definitions of what it means to be a Christian can vary widely depending on whom you talk to.

So it is imperative that we understand what being a Christian means and how to relay that to others. Before we go on, write out *your* definition of Christianity and take the Christianity Pop Quiz.

1. Being a Christian means

_____

_____

_____

_____

_____

_____

2. Christianity Pop Quiz

T F I will go to heaven if I am good
enough.

T F Anyone can believe in Jesus.

T F I can accept Jesus without coming
to Him for forgiveness.

T F Jesus is just a great alternative to
life's problems.

T F I can be a Christian without a
change in my lifestyle.

Christianity as a Lifestyle

Being a Christian means more than receiving help from a higher power. Being a Christian is more than spending a few hours in church each week.

Christianity is a lifestyle that you choose by accepting Christ as your Savior. You're not born into it. You can't earn it. You can't catch it as you can a cold or the flu. You must sincerely and consciously choose to become a Christian by receiving God's gift of forgiveness that He offers us through the Cross.

The Christian life, then, is a journey. It begins when we accept Christ as our Savior. It's a journey in which we practice faith and obedience. We are to demonstrate Christ in our lives and become more like Him.

A subtle but powerful tool of Satan's is to lull us to sleep with the notion that Jesus is just there to help us cope with the problems of life.

We keep Him around to comfort and help us, but we don't get too crazy about actually adopting His teachings.

In reality, Christ desires to work in our lives in a powerful way and transform them into something exciting and meaningful. Let's turn to the Bible to identify what God's Word says about being a Christian.

When was the word "Christian" used for the first time? In Acts 11:26 we find the answer to this question. "The disciples were first called Christians in Antioch." So what was so special about Antioch?

We can find that out by reading verses 11 through 30. Some Jews who believed in Jesus left Jerusalem, went to Antioch, and there started telling people about Christ. Verse 21 tells us, "The hand of the Lord was with them, and a large number who believed turned to the Lord."

The lives of the people in Antioch must have begun to change dramatically, because the church all the way back in Jerusalem heard about what was going on there and sent Barnabas to check it out.

When Barnabas arrived, he saw the "grace of God" in the people of Antioch, and he rejoiced (v. 23). And verse 24 says that then even more people became Christians. It sounds as if these people's Christianity was spreading like wildfire. It was this transformation of lives that first prompted others to call those disciples of Christ *Christians*.

We also know that this name for Christ's followers must have become common, because later, in Acts 26, even a king knew the term. Here Paul is telling King Agrippa what Christ has done in his life. When Paul finishes his story, King Agrippa says, "In a short time you will persuade me to become a Christian" (v. 28).

If even a pagan king was familiar with the term—as well as the conversion process needed to become a Christian—it is not surprising that *Christian* should become the name most recognized by all people to signify a follower of Christ.

Just the facts (so how does someone become a Christian?). The first step in becoming a Christian is to recognize that we have all done wrong things. Romans 3:23 says, "For all have sinned and fall short of the glory of God."

Sin entered the world when Adam disobeyed God in the Garden of Eden. Since then, all of us have been born with a nature that is self-serving and rebellious. Because of this sin nature, people lie, steal, cheat, and murder to get what they want, and none of us lives the righteous and God-centered life for which we were designed.

Our sin nature falls so short of God's holiness that He cannot have a relationship with us. Our sin stands in the way. That is why He sent Jesus, His only Son, into the world.

Jesus wasn't like us. Because He was God, He was perfect. He did not sin. Because He was perfect, He was able to become a sacrifice for *our* sins when He died on the cross.

Romans 5:6–8 says: "For while we were still helpless, at the right time Christ died for the ungodly. For one will hardly die for a righteous man. . . . But God demonstrates His own love toward us, in that while we were yet sinners, Christ died for us."

Because Jesus died as a sacrifice for our sins, our relationship with God can be restored. Romans 6:23 says, "For the wages of sin is death, but the free gift of God is eternal life in Christ Jesus our Lord."

All we have to do is receive Jesus' gift of forgiveness and eternal life by believing in Him—that is, accepting Him as our Savior. John 3:16 says, "For God so loved the world, that He gave His only begotten Son, that whoever believes in Him should not perish, but have eternal life."

And Romans 10:9 tells us, "If you confess with your mouth Jesus as Lord, and believe in your heart that God raised Him from the dead, you shall be saved."

In him we have redemption through his blood, the forgiveness of sins, in accordance with the riches of God's grace that he lavished on us with all wisdom and understanding.
Ephesians 1:7–8 (NIV)

But can't people save themselves by doing good? Ephesians 2:8–9 says, "For by grace you have been saved through faith; and that not of yourselves, it is the gift of God; not as a result of works, that no one should boast."

It is only by God's grace that we can be saved from our sins and from eternity in hell. Grace is God's giving to us His personal forgiveness even though we don't deserve it.

Because God is completely righteous, doing even one thing wrong disqualifies us from a relationship with Him. And it is only through the gift of the one Man who was completely perfect that a relationship with God can be restored and we can be admitted into heaven.

But can Jesus save us from a sinful future here on earth? Romans 8:1–2 says: "There is therefore now no condemnation for those who are in Christ Jesus. For the law of the Spirit of life in Christ Jesus has set you free from the law of sin and of death."

When you accept Christ as your Savior, your slate is wiped clean. You are forgiven of all your sins. In addition, although you may still do wrong things, you no longer have to be a slave to sin because Christ has set you free.

"Therefore if any man is in Christ, he is a new creature; the old things passed away; behold, new things have come" (2 Corinthians 5:17). Christians are a new creation, designed to do good works instead of the self-serving evil that was so much a part of us before.

"We are His workmanship," Ephesians 2:10 says, "created in Christ Jesus for good works, which God prepared beforehand, that we should walk in them." God prepared good works for us to do before we were even born.

So what is our relationship with Jesus like after we become Christians?
Hebrews 2:17–18 says:

> Therefore, He had to be made like His brethren in all things, that He might become a merciful and faithful high priest in things pertaining to God, to make propitiation for the sins of the people. For since He Himself was tempted in that which He has suffered, He is able to come to the aid of those who are tempted.

Jesus can relate physically, emotionally, and mentally to us because He lived the life of a man on earth. That word *propitiation* in the verse above literally means "a peace offering," so, when we accept Christ, He becomes our continual peace offering to God for our sins. And since He was tempted during His life on earth, when *we* are tempted, He is able to help us through the power of His Holy Spirit whom He sends to live in each of us.

In addition, after we become Christians, we are adopted into God's family. Paul explains this in Romans 8:14–17:

> For all who are being led by the Spirit of God, these are sons of God. For you have . . . received a spirit of adoption as sons by which we cry out, "Abba! Father!" The Spirit Himself

bears witness with our spirit that we are children of God, and if children, heirs also, heirs of God and fellow heirs with Christ, if indeed we suffer with Him in order that we may also be glorified with Him.

So not only is Jesus our peace offering and help during temptation, but He also becomes a brother to us. After we receive Him, we are a part of the spiritual family of God, heirs to God's eternal riches along with Christ. We are able to approach Him and call Him Father, and we are able to call Jesus our friend and brother.

Then what's the big deal about going to church? When we accept Christ, we not only become children of God and joint heirs with Christ, but we also become part of a family with all the other believers in the world. Romans 12:4–5 explains that Christians are all one "body" in Christ. Each of us individually has a special function that is important to the body as a whole, just as each part of our physical bodies has a special function. Becoming involved in a church is the way we hook up with the rest of the body.

Hebrews 10:25 says that we should not forsake "our own assembling together." Meeting with other Christians helps us grow. Interaction with other believers can encourage us, challenge us, and help us learn more about God. In addition, church also gives us the opportunity to serve and to be involved in what God is doing in the world. As a whole body we can do things that we could never accomplish as individuals.

Because we are all one family in Christ, Christians should be committed to loving each other regardless of any difference in race, culture, opinions, or talents. Romans 12:10 tells us to "be devoted to one another in brotherly love," and 1 Peter 1:22 instructs us to "fervently love one another from the heart." Assembling with other believers gives us the opportunity to live out these commandments.

So Now, One More Time!
What Is Christianity?

Christianity, then, is living by faith in Christ Jesus one day at a time. It is applying His teachings to our lives and being a part of all God's wonderful works that He planned for us ahead of time. It is joining God in carrying out His will and purpose for the world.

For I am confident of this very thing, that He who began a good work in you will perfect it until the day of Christ Jesus.
Philippians 1:6

Let's Put Our Christianity into Practice

Being a Christian means living differently from those who are not Christians. But how do we put our Christianity into practice? Below is a list of verses that gives us some instruction on how to become more Christlike. Read each passage and write a short summary of the guidance it gives.

Proverbs 3:5–6

_____

_____

Ephesians 4:29–32

_____

_____

Philippians 2:3–4

_____

_____

Colossians 3:16–17

_____

_____

1 Thessalonians 5:21

_____

_____

2 Timothy 2:15

_____

_____

Titus 2:6–8

_____

_____

James 1:2–4

_____

James 5:16

_____

_____

1 John 1:9

_____

_____

SELF-EVALUATION

Rate yourself in the following areas using a scale from 1 to 10, with 1 being the weakest and 10 being perfect.

_____ I am positive that I am a Christian.

_____ I have totally committed my life to Jesus Christ.

_____ I am able to communicate to others what it means to be a Christian.

_____ I am actively trying to share the message of Christ with others.

_____ I am constantly striving to become more like Christ.

_____ I am committed to being an active part of a church.

_____ I respect and love other Christians regardless of their denomination, culture, or race.

Write a paragraph below describing the kind of Christian you would like to be.

_____

_____

_____

_____

_____

_____

_____

_____

_____

_____

STEPPING OUT TOMORROW WITH CHRIST

As we leave today, we face the same old world tomorrow. Friends, teachers, parents, coaches, and so on will all be there, ready for another interaction with us. What will be different about the way we interact with these people?

It's time to make a promise to God.

We have discussed the topic of Christianity. What commitment would God have you make regarding the things we talked about today? Was there something you read that is tugging at your mind? If so, there is a good chance that God is trying to focus your attention.

Think over the Self-Evaluation carefully. Ask Him what specific promise He would have you make. After you have decided what your promise will be, write it on the next page and then write three action steps that will help you fulfill this promise.

I promise:

_____

_____

_____

_____

_____

_____

Three action steps that will help me keep my promise:

1. _____

_____

_____

_____

2. _____

_____

_____

_____

3. _____

_____

_____

_____

Memory Verse : Ephesians 2:8–10

OPTIONAL GROUP ACTIVITIES

A. Between now and the next meeting, conduct a mini-survey of three to five people from among your friends or acquaintances. Ask each person the question, "What does it mean to be a Christian?" Record their answers and bring them with you to the next meeting.

B. Take one of the Scripture references listed under the section entitled "Let's Put Our Christianity into Practice" and think about how the guidance provided in that verse can help you in your everyday life. Make a list of practical examples and bring it with you to the next meeting. Feel free to use Bible commentaries or to ask other people for their opinions on the verse.

Promise 2

DEVELOPING SELF-RESPECT

Scott was outgoing and had lots of friends. He had a great sense of humor that attracted others to him. For the most part, Scott seemed to have his act together, but sometimes he did stretch the truth a little, especially when that would make him the center of attention.

As Scott grew older, his little lies began getting bigger and bigger. It was as if he couldn't just tell the truth; he had to embellish it to impress people and get bigger laughs. He even began using his storytelling to get himself out of trouble.

When Terry, Scott's best friend since grade school, finally confronted him about his tall tales, Scott got angry and even suggested that Terry was just jealous of his popularity. Terry dropped the subject, but he was afraid that Scott's obvious lack of self-respect would destroy their friendship and lead to big problems for Scott in the future.

THE BASIS FOR OUR SELF-RESPECT

Then God said, "Let Us make man in Our image, according to Our likeness; and let them rule over the fish of the sea and over the birds of the sky and over the cattle and over all the earth, and over every creeping thing that creeps on the earth." And God created man in His own image, in the image of God He created him; male and female He created them.

Genesis 1:26–27

Read the above passage slowly and consider the implications of these verses. Just think—we are made in the very image of God! That's hard to comprehend, but it means that in our basic makeup we must possess some of the very characteristics of God Himself. We are also told again and again in the Bible how much God loves us and how much He has been willing to do for us. Since all of these things are true, shouldn't we have more respect for ourselves?

Healthy self-respect is acknowledging the truth about how God sees us. It is accepting ourselves as God made us. It is understanding that God has a special purpose for each of us.

Before we go on, write in the space provided what you think is the difference between self-respect and pride.

_____

_____

_____

_____

_____

_____

What are some examples of things a person with self-respect might do?

_____

_____

_____

_____

_____

What are some examples of things a person with pride might do?

_____

_____

_____

_____

_____

What Causes Us to Lose Our Self-Respect?

Did you ever wonder why some people have so little respect for themselves? Let's look at an example from the Bible and see if we can get an understanding of what causes this.

Adam had a great beginning; he was created by God's own hands in the image of God Himself. After this, he walked and talked with God in the Garden of Eden. Then one evening when God came to the garden to spend time with him, Adam tried to hide.

Read Genesis 3:6–10. What caused Adam to lose so much self-respect that he thought it necessary to hide from God?

_____

_____

_____

_____

_____

_____

_____

Nothing makes us lose respect for ourselves faster than sin does. Sin drives a wedge between us and God and inhibits our fellowship with Him. Since healthy self-respect is based on understanding our position in Christ, our self-respect suffers when our relationship with God is damaged by sin—especially when there is recurring sin that we have been unable to gain control over. Recurring sin tends to start a cycle causing more sin, because, when our self-respect is damaged, we are even more vulnerable to temptation.

Having sisters who always do better than we do or having friends who are always putting us down can challenge our self-respect. But if our self-respect is based on our position in Christ, the only thing that can really harm it is something that damages our relationship with Him.

If you have an area of recurring sin in your life, take whatever steps are necessary to gain control of that area *now*. This may mean doing something drastic to remove yourself from the situation. It may require telling someone else about the problem you are having and asking that person to keep you accountable. Whatever it takes, make sure that you do not accept sin as a permanent fixture in your life.

Mirror, Mirror, on the Wall

The things we do are always based on what we think. If you think you aren't pretty, you probably won't enter a beauty contest. If you think the guy who sits next to you in geometry is a serial killer, you probably won't hang around with him.

And what we think *about ourselves* powerfully influences what we do. We will most likely act in a way that is consistent with our view of who we are. That is why it's important that we make sure our self-concept matches up with God's truth of who we really are in Him.

Before we can change any of our thinking, however, we must take a deep look at what we truly believe about ourselves. Take a minute to consider how you honestly see yourself. Then write down some of those perceptions in the space below. In order for this exercise to be helpful, you must be as honest as possible.

When I look at myself I see:

1. _____

_____

_____

2. _____

_____

_____

3. _____

_____

_____

4. _____

_____

_____

5. _____

_____

_____

Next, imagine that you need to let someone who has never met you know what you are truly like. Write a paragraph below showing how you would describe yourself to this person. Tell about both your internal and external characteristics.

_____

_____

_____

_____

_____

_____

_____

_____

_____

_____

_____

_____

_____

_____

_____

_____

_____

How Does God See You?

We have just completed some exercises about how we see ourselves; now let's take a look at how God sees us. Look up the following verses and write beside them what they say you truly are, according to Him.

Matthew 5:13–14: I am

_____

_____

John 15:15: I am

_____

_____

Romans 8:15–17: I am

_____

_____

1 Corinthians 3:16–19: I am

_____

_____

1 Corinthians 6:15: I am

_____

_____

1 Corinthians 12:7–11: I am

_____

_____

_____

2 Corinthians 5:17: I am

_____

_____

2 Corinthians 5:18–19: I am

_____

_____

Ephesians 2:10: I am

_____

_____

Philippians 3:20: I am

_____

_____

Colossians 3:12: I am

_____

_____

1 Peter 2:9–10: I am

_____

_____

1 John 3:1–2: I am

_____

_____

Though we may not realize it, God sees us as all those things! He has given us a new position in Christ, and He sees in us the potential to be the men and women that He desires us to be. What we need to do to take advantage of

43

these powerful truths is to realize who we are in Christ and commit ourselves to act accordingly by the power of the Holy Spirit.

Signs of Someone Without Self-Respect

Many times it is easy to spot a man or woman with little self-respect. Even people who do a good job of covering their lack of self-respect eventually give little evidences that reveal their true view of themselves. The following are common indicators of poor self-respect:

- Cheating on a test
- Taking credit when credit isn't due
- Lying to cover up a mistake
- Abusing drugs
- Making decisions based solely on what peers think
- Being desperate to have a girlfriend or boyfriend
- Being unable to walk away from a bad situation
- Taking part in a sexual relationship before marriage
- Failing to care for one's own body and health

In the space below, list any other signs of poor self-respect that you can think of.

_____

_____

_____

_____

_____

_____

_____

_____

_____

_____

_____

_____

_____

_____

Now go back through the above list and mark the items that you have noticed in your life recently. If you often have problems with any of these areas, that may be a sign that you are having trouble seeing yourself as God sees you and respecting yourself for who God made you to be. If so, this could be an area you need to work on.

Models of Godly Men and Women

God very much wants us to live up to our potential and His plan for us. He intends for us to act, talk, and serve in ways that are pleasing to Him.

Listed below are some examples of godly people in the Bible. Remember that these individuals were human just like you. The thing that set them apart was their commitment to be true to God. Write down some of the godly character traits that each displayed.

Deborah: Judge of a Nation (Read Judges 4–5.)

_____

_____

_____

_____

_____

Joseph: Egypt's GQ Man of the Year (Read Genesis 39.)

_____

_____

_____

_____

_____

Ruth: Tragedy to Triumph: A Real Cinderella Story (Read Ruth 1–4.)

_____

_____

_____

_____

Joshua: A Man Against All Odds (Read Joshua 24:1–18.)

_____

_____

_____

_____

_____

Abigail: First Nobel Peace Prize Winner (Read 1 Samuel 25:2–38.)

_____

_____

_____

_____

_____

Shadrach, Meshach, Abednego: The Original Three Musketeers (Read Daniel 3.)

_____

_____

_____

_____

_____

Mary: Mother of the King of Kings (Read Luke 1:26–2:52.)

_____

_____

_____

_____

_____

Timothy: The First Promise Maker (Read 1 Timothy 4:12–16.)

_____

_____

_____

_____

Becoming a Person Worthy of Respect

You already are immeasurably valuable in the eyes of Christ. You are His child, a citizen of heaven, and part of a royal priesthood. God wants to help us live up to our potential. He wants us to be people who mirror God's character. Such a life will build within us self-respect that is based on allowing Jesus Christ to live His purpose and will through our lives. Listed below are some insights into how to become the man or woman God wants you to be:

- Commit to living for Christ (Philippians 1:21).
- Treat others with respect and purity (1 Timothy 5:1–2).
- Honor those in authority over you (1 Peter 2:13–17).
- Demonstrate love to everyone (1 John 4:11).

• Don't be deceived (Colossians 2:8).

Protecting Christ's Image

Does God care what other people think about you? Is He concerned about the image you portray to those you meet? In 1 Corinthians 8, we find an interesting example of how important the image we project to others is to Christ.

These verses deal with a dilemma the people in Corinth were experiencing: Should a Christian eat meat that had been offered to idols?

Of course, the idols were nothing but blocks of wood and stone, so they didn't eat the meat that the pagan people offered them. That meant it was left for others to buy. Some were saying it was OK for Christians to eat this meat, and some were saying that to do so was sin.

Paul ended the argument by telling them that nothing was wrong with eating this meat, because, as the Christians knew, these false gods were only figments of people's imagination. *But,* he said, if someone else didn't realize that and would be hurt in any way by seeing a Christian eat such meat, then the Christian should not eat it.

Paul concluded, "Therefore, if food causes my brother to stumble, I will never eat meat again, that I might not cause my brother to stumble" (v. 13). In other words, the image you portray to other people *is* important because, as a Christian, you represent Christ.

The list below points out a few areas that you may need to look at in regard to demonstrating your self-respect and protecting the image of Christ people see in you.

• Personal Appearance

Make sure you dress in a way that shows respect for yourself and for Christ. Show respect for others by not having bad breath or body odor. Be quick to show Christ's love through a smile.

• Speech and Conduct

Make sure your speech is clean and shows respect for others. Be upbeat and appreciative.

• Approach to Work

No matter what you are doing, do it well and make sure you follow your tasks through to completion. Always look for ways to improve your work, and go the extra mile for your employer.

Keeping a clear conscience, so that those who speak maliciously against your good behavior in Christ may be ashamed of their slander.
1 Peter 3:16 (NIV)

SELF-EVALUATION

Do you have godly respect for yourself, or do you see signs of poor self-respect in your life? Explain.

_____

_____

_____

_____

_____

_____

_____

_____

_____

_____

_____

_____

Do you see yourself as God sees you, or are there things about yourself that you tend to be overly negative about? Explain.

_____

_____

_____

_____

_____

_____

_____

Are there some negative things that are hurting your self-respect, things that you know shouldn't be a part of your life but that you have not been able to gain control over? Explain.

_____

_____

_____

_____

_____

_____

_____

_____

_____

If you listed some areas, what is the next step you need to take to get control over these things?

_____

_____

_____

_____

_____

_____

STEPPING OUT TOMORROW WITH CHRIST

Self-respect is not something you are automatically born with. Adam and Eve may have had it from their first breath, but when sin came on the scene, they had to rebuild their self-respect from the ground up. You and I need to work daily at seeing ourselves as God sees us. Self-respect begins with aligning ourselves with

God's thinking and ends with letting Him work through our lives.

Your promise below should reflect your commitment to build respect for yourself by beginning to view yourself as God views you. Pray about this promise and then write it down along with three practical steps that you can take to help support this promise.

I promise:

_____

_____

_____

_____

_____

_____

Three action steps that will help me keep my promise:

1. _____

_____

_____

_____

2. _____

_____

_____

_____

3. _____

_____

_____

_____

Memory Verse: Proverbs 3:5–6

Optional Group Activities

A. At the end of each day for the next week, think over the things you did that day. Replay conversations that you had or situations that you reacted to and determine what level of self-respect you showed. Write down anything that you did that demonstrated either godly self-respect or poor self-respect. Bring your insights to the meeting next time to share with the group.

B. Look over the list in the "Models of Godly Men and Women" section. Can you find some ways in which you can relate to these people? Can you see God developing in you some of the traits they demonstrated? List some of the strengths and weaknesses in your spiritual life. Then go back and write down how God might use each of those strengths and weaknesses to mold you into the Christian man or woman He wants you to be. Bring your lists to the next meeting to discuss with the group.

WOMEN, DATING, AND RESPECT

Brett really liked Jennifer. She was beautiful, smart, and fun to be around. And she seemed to like spending time with him. Brett finally mustered up his courage to ask her out.

However, when he called, Jennifer asked all sorts of questions, such as where they would be going, who they would be with, and when she would be home.

Brett was confused. Why was she asking all these questions? Didn't she trust him? He answered her questions, but he still thought she was rude to interrogate him. Maybe he had been wrong about her.

But when Brett mentioned his concerns to his youth leader, the youth leader suggested that maybe Jennifer respected herself and was just wanting to make sure that Brett was also going to respect her on their date—and that that might be a good sign about Jennifer, instead of a bad one.

KEYS TO HEALTHY RELATIONSHIPS WITH WOMEN

Many men have fallen when it came to the area of women and dating. The temptations are strong, and the messages we receive from those around us often undermine the teaching we have received in Sunday school. Even some supposedly religious organizations are now echoing the message we hear in the world.

But it *is* possible to remain pure, and it is crucial to your walk as a Christian. Not following God's instruction in this area can seriously damage your life for years to come. Contracting a sexually transmitted disease, becoming a father before you are ready, and scarring yourself emotionally and spiritually are only some of the consequences.

Viewing our own bodies in the way that God would have us view them is the first step to becoming victorious; the second step is understanding how God would have us view women.

Respecting God's temples. First Corinthians 6:19–20 says: "Or do you not know that your body is a temple of the Holy Spirit who is in you . . . and that you are not your own? For you have been bought with a price: therefore glorify God in your body."

Since your body is the temple of the Holy Spirit, you don't want to do anything that will

56

defile it. God created sexual relationships to be enjoyed within the marriage context alone. Anything other than that is a perversion of His plan, a defilement of God's temple, and a source of destruction to you spiritually.

First Thessalonians 4:3–4 reads: "For this is the will of God, your sanctification; that is, that you abstain from sexual immorality; that each of you know how to possess his own vessel in sanctification and honor." It doesn't get much plainer than that. God wants you to keep yourself pure regarding sexual relationships outside of marriage.

We need to recognize something else in these verses. These verses were written to both men and women. That means that not only are our bodies temples of God, but also women's bodies are temples of God. If we indulge in sexual relationships outside of marriage, not only are we defiling our own temple, but, if this involves a Christian woman, we are being instrumental in defiling her temple also. And if she is not a Christian, we are being a stumbling block to her coming to Christ and becoming His temple.

We are to glorify God in our bodies. What are some ways men can do this?

_____

_____

_____

_____

_____

Since this passage also applies to women, what are some ways we can help the women we know glorify God?

_____

_____

_____

_____

_____

_____

Understanding God's view of women. In Genesis 2:18, God says that it was not good for man to be alone. That is why He made women. They hold a special role in God's creation, just as men do. And we can see in both the Old and New Testaments that women have played an important part in His plan throughout history.

Much of Scripture's instruction on the relationship between men and women is marriage-based. Since dating as we know it was not practiced in Bible times, there may seem to be a shortage of specific dating advice. However, in the instruction provided for marriage situations, we can often get an understanding of how God views men and women that can be translated to the dating situation.

First Peter 3:7 is an example of this. Here, the husband is instructed to treat his wife with honor as a fellow heir of the grace of life. That means women are fellow—or equal—heirs with us in Christ's kingdom. In this same verse, the woman is also referred to as a "vessel." The word *vessel* suggests something of high value. In other words, women are of high value in God's sight, and we need to treat them in that way.

First Thessalonians 5:11 says: "Therefore encourage one another, and build up one another." This verse is important in understanding how we are to treat the women in our lives. We are to do whatever we can to help them grow closer to God. That applies to every woman in our lives, including sisters, friends, and girl-friends. If we constantly keep this as the top priority in every relationship we have with a woman, everything else should fall in line.

For all of you who were baptized into Christ have clothed yourselves with Christ. There is neither Jew nor Greek, there is neither slave nor free man, there is neither male nor female; for you are all one in Christ Jesus.
Galatians 3:27–28

DATING

Having the proper view of yourself and of women is the basis for godly dating. Dating can be a very positive experience, but it can also involve pitfalls. Who you date and the relationships you allow to develop through dating will have a strong impact on your life.

Always remember that the person you

marry will come from the pool of girls you date. Think about that. It's probably a safe bet that you will never marry someone you never dated. Agreed? Then, since you will marry someone from the pool of those you do date, it is imperative that you pick those women carefully.

Put another way, when you choose to date a certain woman, you are putting yourself in danger of marrying her someday. Many men have started dating women they knew God would not have them marry—without any intention of ever marrying them. However, after dating for a prolonged period, they have fallen in love with them and have been unwilling to break off the relationship. Ten years later, they wonder how they ever wound up married to a woman who doesn't desire to serve Christ.

Another reason to choose carefully the girl you date is that dating someone who doesn't hold the same convictions you do about purity will almost invariably cause you to stumble concerning those convictions. Sexual temptation is strong, and, when the person you are dating isn't committed to helping you hold to your convictions, it becomes increasingly difficult to stick to your standards. The converse is also true. If the person you are dating *is* committed to purity, that gives *you* added strength.

This doesn't necessarily mean you can't go get a Coke with a girl you wouldn't want to marry, or that you can't be friends with all kinds of girls. However, you should definitely consider these things before you become involved in any serious dating relationship.

Men choose who they will date for many different reasons. Some of those reasons are good and honorable, and some of them aren't. Unfortunately, the following are some common faulty reasons men have for choosing the women they date:

- To impress others
- To make someone else jealous
- To build up their ego
- To control another person
- To rebel against their parents or friends

List any others you can think of:

_____

_____

_____

_____

_____

_____

_____

_____

_____

All of us are highly susceptible to these kinds of motivations, but it is important to examine yourself and make sure that these are not present in your own dating choices.

The Future Mrs. Perfect

Describe the characteristics you would like to have in a wife. Include physical, mental, and spiritual characteristics, as well as any dreams or interests you would like her to have.

_____

_____

_____

_____

_____

_____

_____

_____

_____

_____

Dating has many benefits:

- It helps us develop interpersonal skills.
- It helps us get to know the other person better.
- It helps us become comfortable with someone of the opposite sex.
- It helps us obtain a better understanding of what we like or dislike in a mate.
- It gives us an opportunity to put into practice God's teachings of respect, consideration, and love.
- It usually is a lot of fun.

On the other hand, we need to be aware of the dangers in dating. Some of those dangers are:

- Becoming too physically involved
- Becoming too wrapped up in the dating relationship to care about friends, family, church, and so on
- Getting emotionally attached to someone you know God wouldn't want you to marry

Dating in Action

Remember, we are to encourage and build up others as we interact with them. This attitude should especially be embraced in our dating. Now let's move our words into actions by thinking of some things we can do to glorify God in our dating relationships.

Actions we can take in preparing for the date:

1. _____

_____

_____

2. _____

_____

_____

3. _____

_____

_____

Actions we can take during the date:

1. _____

_____

_____

2. _____

_____

_____

3. _____

_____

_____

Actions we can take at the end of the date or after the date:

1. _____

_____

_____

2. _____

_____

_____

3. _____

_____

_____

Now flee from youthful lusts, and pursue righteousness, faith, love, and peace.
2 Timothy 2:22

Man to Man

It is important that, as Christian men, we take responsibility for the tone of a date and for any relationship we develop with a woman. As Christian men, we need to stand firmly and be accountable to God for our actions in order to live out our faith in our dating relationships. The following are some reminders to help you keep your dating life pure:

- Spend most of your dating time with friends or other couples.
- Do not caress a woman's legs, hips, or breasts.
- If you kiss, keep it short.
- If you become sexually aroused, quickly take action to change the direction things are going.
- Never spend prolonged periods of time in a secluded place by yourselves.
- Keep your clothes on and keep your date's clothes on.

Other things you might consider doing to help guard your dating life:

- Pray with your date at the beginning of each date.
- Discuss spiritual things with your date.
- Pray with your date at the end of each time together instead of kissing each other good night.

It is crucial that you keep your thought life clean. Jesus says in Matthew 5:28 that anyone who looks on a woman to lust for her has already committed adultery with her in his heart. That means if you have lustful thoughts about a woman, you have already sinned. In addition to that, when you allow yourself to entertain sensual thoughts, it becomes much harder for you not to take some action that falls along the same line as those thoughts.

There are many levels of pornography available today. It is almost impossible to live in the world we do without seeing provocative pictures of women. We must guard our minds and our eyes and not allow ourselves to harbor lust. Satan can use any amount of leeway you give him to get you started on a road toward immorality.

Many Christian men have become addicted to pornography through allowing themselves one small indulgence, and the effects have ravaged their lives, their marriages, and their effectiveness for Christ. Do not allow Satan a foothold in your life.

Picking Up the Pieces

1 John 1:9 assures us that God will always forgive us no matter what we have done if we will only come to Him and confess our sin. If you do something to compromise God's standards for sexual purity, seek His forgiveness first and ask Him for His strength to renew your commitment in this area.

Then write down what happened and how you think God would view what you did. Write out a commitment statement to Him, promising not to repeat the sin. If the sin was regarding your actions while with a woman, call her, apologize for what happened, and ask for her forgiveness as well.

When you ask for God's forgiveness, He forgives you totally and makes you clean again by the power of Jesus' blood. It is important that, after you have asked Christ's forgiveness, you also forgive yourself and turn your attention to your present actions and to encouraging and building up anyone else who was affected by what you did.

Sometimes we develop a sinful pattern in which we keep committing the same sin. These patterns can gradually tear us down spiritually and greatly damage our effectiveness as Christians. Many times, something drastic must be done to break the pattern. However, whether it requires you break up with a certain girl or to commit to dating only in a group setting—or even to ask someone else to keep you accountable regarding the problem area—don't ever just accept the sin as part of your life. Through God's power, it is possible to overcome it.

Yet the Lord longs to be gracious to you; he rises to show you compassion.
Isaiah 30:18 (NIV)

ONE MAN'S EXPERIENCE
A TRUE ACCOUNT

I learned about dating and relationships with girls the wrong way—from older teenage boys in my neighborhood. In the summertime, when all of our parents were at work, these boys used to invite me over. I was flattered that they wanted me around, especially when their girlfriends were at their houses. However, I soon found out that they only invited me over because they thought it was funny to expose me to masturbation, pornography, and their sexual relationships with girls.

I didn't realize it at the time, but what these guys exposed me to had an impact on my attitudes toward girls. As I got older, I found myself drawn to the girls who liked sexual advances and innuendos.

Fortunately, God brought a Christian girl into my life at that time who was strong in her convictions about being pure. She introduced me to a relationship with Jesus Christ and communicated the importance of sexual purity to me. While I found her standards difficult at first, I was drawn to her. The Holy Spirit convicted me of my improper conduct and provided a foundation for standards about purity that then guided me throughout high school and college dating.

But for a time, I was an example of the Garbage In, Garbage Out concept. I did not have a proper view of myself or of women because I'd learned my standards from the wrong crowd. I am fortunate that someone cared enough about me to show me how to honor myself and the women I dated. I hate to think how things might have turned out had not that person come along. I pray that you will not follow the same route I started down as a teenager, and I thank God I was able to escape from it by His power.

SELF-EVALUATION

Rate yourself in the following areas using a scale from 1 to 10, with 1 being the weakest and 10 being perfect.

_____ I generally show purity and respect for women in what I say.

_____ I realize that I defile my own body, which is the temple of God, when I am sexually impure.

_____ I generally encourage and build up the women I am around.

_____ I have established clear standards and

69

guidelines in my dating life.

_____ I keep my mind free from lustful thoughts.

_____ I have not allowed pornography to have a foothold in my life.

_____ I am committed to doing whatever is necessary to rid my life of any pattern of sin that develops.

What are some changes you need to make in your dating life and other relationships with women?

_____

_____

_____

_____

_____

_____

STEPPING OUT TOMORROW WITH CHRIST

Women are just as important in this life as men. We need to view them as God would have us view them and respect them in our speech and actions. Women do not owe men anything. They are not required to submit to every man in their lives. Any submission that takes place is between a married couple, and even that submission is a two-way experience.

The way we conduct ourselves when dating is important and can have lasting effects. We need to set standards for ourselves regarding whom we will date and how we will conduct ourselves on those dates. And we need to guard our thoughts and our actions against sexual impurity.

Commitments made now about how we will view and treat women will stay with us all our lives. If we embrace God's view of women and God's plan for sexual relationships, we will be able to enjoy the relationships we have with women without guilt, and we will keep ourselves pure for service to God. Write out your commitment below, and then write three action steps that you can take to help keep that commitment.

I promise:

_____

_____

_____

_____

_____

_____

Three action steps that will help me keep my promise:

1. _____

_____

_____

_____

2. _____

_____

_____

_____

3. _____

_____

_____

_____

Memory Verse: 1 Thessalonians 5:11

OPTIONAL GROUP ACTIVITIES

A. Sometime between now and the next meeting, talk with a Christian friend who is a girl and ask her what kinds of things she thinks Christian girls are looking for in the guys they date. Choose someone who will be honest and objective (preferably someone you are not in a dating relationship with). Take notes on what she says and bring them with you to the next meeting to discuss.

B. Think over the things that we have considered in this section and develop a written list of standards for your dating life. Be specific, and be sure to consider ways that you can prevent any bad situations from happening in the first place. Bring your list to the next meeting for discussion.

Promise 3 (b)

MEN, DATING, AND RESPECT

Nichole's parents had said she could start dating when she turned sixteen, but she didn't see any guys flocking to her door after her birthday. There were only three guys around her age in her church, and they were all dating other girls. To make things worse, her friends were beginning to tease her about her datelessness. Nichole was beginning to wish that she had never turned sixteen so that she would at least have an excuse for never having had a date when someone finally called to ask her out.

Nichole hadn't been able to believe it when the voice on the phone said he was Shane Bradley and that he wanted to ask her out. Shane was a basketball player and one of the best-looking guys in her school. Unfortunately, Nichole knew he wasn't a Christian.

She hesitated, realizing that this was the

chance of a lifetime. It would be great to be seen with Shane, and then maybe some other guys would notice her and ask her out. But on the other hand, she had made a commitment to date only Christian guys. Besides, from what she had heard, Shane wasn't really the kind of guy she would want a relationship with anyway.

Nichole took a deep breath and then told Shane that she was sorry but she couldn't go out with him. Even as she heard the words coming from her mouth, she couldn't believe that she was actually going to turn him down. Everybody at school would think that it was the stupidest thing she had ever done—if they even believed that he had asked her out in the first place.

KEYS TO HEALTHY RELATIONSHIPS WITH GUYS

Although dating can be a positive experience, it also can often be difficult and confusing. The decisions you make regarding dating and relationships with people of the opposite sex can have far-reaching and devastating effects on your life and on your effectiveness for Christ.

The temptations in this area are some of the strongest temptations that many of us will ever face, and the messages we receive from those around us often undermine the teaching we have received at home and in Sunday school. Even some supposedly religious organizations are now echoing the message we hear from the world.

But it *is* possible to remain pure and have

rewarding and satisfying dating experiences. However, to do this we must trust God and follow the instructions He has given us for these kinds of relationships. Contracting a sexually transmitted disease, becoming a mother before you are ready, and scarring yourself and others emotionally and spiritually are only some of the consequences of not following God's teachings in this area.

Respecting God's temples. First Corinthians 6:19–20 says: "Do you not know that your body is a temple of the Holy Spirit who is in you, whom you have from God, and that you are not your own? For you have been bought with a price: therefore glorify God in your body."

Since your body is the temple of the Holy Spirit, you don't want to do anything with that temple to defile it. God created sexual relationships to be enjoyed within the marriage context only. Anything outside of that is a perversion of His plan, a defilement of God's temple, and a source of destruction to you spiritually.

In 1 Thessalonians 4:3–4 we read: "This is the will of God, your sanctification; that is, that you abstain from sexual immorality; that each of you know how to possess his own vessel in sanctification and honor." It doesn't get much plainer than that. God wants you to keep yourself pure regarding sexual relationships outside of marriage.

If the body of each Christian is the temple of God, we also need to recognize that any inappropriate relationship we allow to develop between ourselves and a Christian guy not only defiles ourselves as God's temple but also defiles *him* as a temple of God. And if we allow an inappropriate relationship to develop between us and a guy who is not a Christian, we are allowing ourselves to be a stumbling block to that person's coming to Christ and becoming God's temple.

First Corinthians 6:19–20 says that we should glorify God with our bodies. List some ways women can do this:

_____

_____

_____

_____

_____

_____

That verse also applies to men. What are some things we can do to help the guys we know glorify God?

_____

_____

_____

_____

_____

_____

_____

The importance of mutual respect. Respect plays a crucial part in developing healthy relationships with people of the opposite sex.

First Thessalonians 5:11 says, "Therefore encourage one another, and build up one another." This verse applies to everyone in our lives, including those we are dating or interested in dating. Our number one priority in all relationships should be to encourage and build up the other person in Christ. If we keep this in focus, most other things will fall in line.

Write down one potential dating problem and some ideas about how having this focus will help in that situation.

_____

_____

_____

_____

_____

_____

While having a godly respect for others is important in dating relationships, having a godly respect for ourselves is just as important. In chapter 2 we talked extensively about self-respect. Developing this area of your Christian life will greatly improve your potential for healthy dating relationships.

Understanding that your worth comes from Christ, and not from what others think of you, can empower you to make healthy decisions in regard to dating. Never date anyone who does not respect you as God would have him respect you, and don't let anyone manipulate you into doing something that is wrong in order to gain that person's love or approval. Any decisions that you make based on a lack of respect for yourself will always make you ashamed later on and will tear down your spiritual strength.

Can you think of some poor dating choices you have made because of a lack of self-respect? Explain.

_____

_____

_____

_____

_____

_____

DATING

Having the proper respect for yourself and for others is the basis for godly dating. God is the one who designed men and women for relationships with each other, and you can glorify Him through the dating choices you make. Remember that whom you date and the relationships you allow to develop through dating will have a strong impact on your life.

And don't forget that the person you marry will come from the pool of guys you date. Think about that. It's probably a safe bet that you will never marry someone you never dated—right? Then, since you will almost certainly marry someone from the pool of those you date, it is imperative that you pick those people carefully.

Let's put it another way. When you choose to date a certain guy, you are putting yourself in danger of marrying him someday. That may sound a little dramatic, but many women have started dating someone they knew God would not have them marry, without any intention of ever marrying him. However, after dating for a prolonged period of time, they have fallen in love with that person and been unwilling to break off the relationship. Ten years later, they wonder how they ever wound up married to a man who has no desire to serve Christ.

Another reason to pick the guys you date carefully is that dating someone who doesn't hold the same convictions you do about purity will almost invariably cause you to stumble concerning those convictions. Sexual temptation is strong, and when the person you are dating isn't committed to helping you hold to your convictions, it becomes increasingly difficult to stick to your standards. The converse is also true. If the person you are dating *is* committed to purity, that gives *you* added strength.

This doesn't necessarily mean you can't go for a Coke with a guy you wouldn't want to marry, or that you can't be friends with all kinds of guys. However, you should definitely consider these things before you become involved in any serious dating relationship.

Dating Motivations

Women choose whom they will date for many different reasons. Some reasons are good and honoring to God, and some of them aren't. The following is a list of some common faulty reasons women have for choosing whom they date:

- To impress others
- To make someone else jealous
- To build up their self-esteem
- To control another person
- To rebel against their parents or friends

List any other faulty reasons you can think of:

_____

_____

_____

_____

_____

_____

_____

_____

All of us are susceptible to these kinds of motivations, but we need to begin recognizing and rejecting them. Go back and mark any of the above that have motivated you in past dating decisions.

The Future Mr. Perfect

In the space provided, describe some characteristics you would like to have in a husband. Include physical, spiritual, and mental characteristics, as well as any dreams or interests you would like for him to have.

_____

_____

_____

_____

_____

_____

_____

Dating offers many benefits:

- It helps us develop interpersonal skills.
- It helps us get to know the other person better.
- It helps us become comfortable with someone of the opposite sex.
- It helps us obtain a better understanding of what we like or dislike in a mate.
- It gives us an opportunity to practice God's teachings of respect, consideration, and love.
- It usually is a lot of fun.

On the other hand, there are some important dangers in dating that we need to be aware of. Some of those dangers are:

- Becoming too physically involved
- Becoming too wrapped up in the dating relationship to care about friends, family, or church
- Getting emotionally attached to someone you know God wouldn't want you to marry

Dating in Action

Since we are to encourage and build up others as we interact with them, we should embrace this attitude in our dating. Let's now move our words into actions by thinking of some things we can do before the date, during the date, and at the end of the date or after the date that will help us glorify God in our dating.

Actions we can take in preparing for the date:

1. _____

_____

_____

2. _____

_____

_____

3. _____
_____
_____

Actions we can take during the date:

1. _____
_____
_____

2. _____
_____
_____

3. _____
_____
_____

Actions we can take at the end of the date or after the date:

1. _____
_____
_____

2. _____
_____
_____

3. _____

_____

_____

Straight Talk

It's important that we take responsibility for ourselves in dating relationships. We need to decide what our standards are and hold firmly to those standards. The following are some physical reminders to help you keep your dating life pure:

- Spend most of your dating time with friends or other couples.
- Do not allow your date to caress your thighs, hips, or breasts, and do not touch your date in any inappropriate way.
- If you kiss, keep it short.
- Never spend prolonged periods of time in a secluded place by yourselves.
- Never take off any of your clothes or any of your date's clothes.

Some other things you might consider doing to help keep your dating life pure are:

- Pray with your date at the beginning of each date.
- Discuss spiritual things with your date.
- Pray with your date at the end of each

time together instead of kissing each other good night.

It's also important to keep your thought life clean. Jesus says in Matthew 5:28 that any man who looks on a woman to lust for her has committed adultery with her already in his heart. But women are susceptible to lustful thoughts too, and this principle also applies to us. If you allow yourself to entertain lustful thoughts about someone, you have committed sin already. In addition to this, when you allow yourself to entertain lustful thoughts, it becomes much harder for you not to allow actions that fall along the same lines as those thoughts.

Pornography abounds for both men and women. It's almost impossible to live in today's world without seeing provocative pictures, and many books and movies also contain material that makes us think lustfully. We must guard our minds and our eyes and not allow Satan a foothold.

Picking Up the Pieces

First John 1:9 assures us that God will always forgive us no matter what we have done if only we will come to Him and confess our sin. If you do something to compromise God's standards for sexual purity, seek His forgiveness first and ask Him for His strength in renewing your commitment in this area.

It often helps to write out what happened and how you think God views what you did.

Consider writing a commitment statement to God promising not to repeat the sin. If the sin is in regard to actions while on a date, talk to your date about what happened and apologize for your part in the sin.

When you ask for God's forgiveness, He forgives you totally and makes you clean again by the power of Jesus' blood. It's important that, after you have asked His forgiveness, you also forgive yourself and turn your attention to your present actions and to building up anyone else who was affected by what you did.

Sometimes we develop sinful patterns in certain areas of our lives, areas where we keep committing the same sin. These patterns can gradually tear us down spiritually and greatly damage our effectiveness as Christians. Many times we must do something drastic to break the pattern. However, whether it requires you to break up with a certain guy, to commit to dating only in a group setting, or even to ask someone else to keep you accountable regarding that area, don't ever just accept the sin as part of your life. Through God's power, it *is* possible to overcome it.

Yet the Lord longs to be gracious to you; he rises to show you compassion.
Isaiah 30:18 (NIV)

ONE WOMAN'S EXPERIENCE
A TRUE ACCOUNT

As a committed Christian determined to

remain sexually pure, I set strict standards for myself before I started dating. And they worked great for a while. I started dating Lance* during my sophomore year, and we had a lot of fun together. However, as the relationship continued to grow, I didn't realize how strong the temptations would become.

As I began to love Lance more, and we began to share our deepest thoughts and dreams, it became more tempting to share our bodies with each other, too. I began compromising some of my standards in small ways. I allowed myself to go into tempting situations, which at first I had been able to handle, and I allowed things to go just a little bit further than I knew they should.

As I started compromising, a small rift began to form between God and me because I knew I was no longer in His perfect will. My feelings also began to change. It was no longer God and I against the temptations, but instead it was Lance and I facing the impossible standards set up by God.

I asked forgiveness each time things went too far, but eventually I just gave up on trying to be totally pure and, instead, became satisfied with not letting things go any further. I failed at that too.

I was still praying for God's help, but I had already blocked God out of that part of my life by accepting a certain level of sin there. I was putting myself in compromising situations, knowing and accepting that I would fail. I had resigned myself to a life of "partial impurity," and now I was relying on my own strength to salvage what purity I had left. And I was failing.

After dating Lance for more than three years, we broke up. I felt as if my world was shattered, and I promised myself that I would never make the same mistakes again with another guy. However, when I started dating Matt* a few months later, I found myself compromising more than ever. I guess once you've done something with one guy, it's hard to feel there is anything sacred to protect in yourself.

It was a roller coaster that I couldn't stop. When I thought about the impurity I was allowing in my life, I couldn't even believe it was me. What had happened to my strong values and my strength to uphold them? My compromises had given Satan a small foothold, and he had taken it and run.

After I accepted the compromises as a permanent part of my life, I denied God the ability to work in that area. I left it up to myself and my weak, sinful nature. And I wasn't strong enough. I don't think anyone is, once he or she starts compromising. I know that God was standing beside me the whole time, pleading with me to let Him take control again. If only I had listened and committed to doing whatever was necessary to regain purity.

Finally, I think God just said, "Stephanie, I have let you go long enough." I became pregnant at the beginning of my second year of college. God had finally put me at a crossroads, and I had to make a choice of whether I would follow Him. For me this was a real wake-up call. I kept saying over and over, "This is not my life!" All my dreams and intentions seemed to have gone up in smoke. How had things gotten so messed up? I had been a good Christian with strong moral values and beliefs, and I had been that way for most of my life. What had happened to it all?

Fortunately, at that point I made the right choice, and, when I did, God was waiting for me with open arms and unimaginable grace and forgiveness. Matt and I chose to marry each other, to raise our baby, and, as best as we could, to love God and follow Him. I began to see how every part of my relationship with God had suffered because of my continual failure in that one area. Now, more than two years later, I am still working to repair the damage, and I am very regretful when I think of how much I could have grown in my relationship with God during all those years of sin. Instead, I regressed.

God has blessed my life, although I'm sure that He had it planned differently. Many of my heartaches were caused by my sin, and I know I have many more to face.

I firmly believe that our weaknesses are passed on to our children, and I can't stand the thought of being a potential contributor to my daughter Ashley's trials and temptations. Every day I am mindful that one day she will realize my failure and that that may somehow lower the expectations that she has for herself. Mostly I *regret that Matt and I cannot be role models to show her that sexual purity is possible with God's strength. Although we both believe that to be true, I'm afraid that our past actions may speak louder to her than our present words.*

*The names in this story have been changed to protect the identity of the writer.

SELF-EVALUATION

Rate yourself in the following areas using a scale from 1 to 10, with 1 being very weak and 10 being perfect.

_____ My dating habits are glorifying to God.

_____ I realize that I defile my own body, which is the temple of God, when I am sexually impure.

_____ I generally encourage and build up the guys I am around.

_____ I show respect for myself in dating situations.

_____ I have established clear standards and guidelines in my dating life.

_____ I keep my mind free from lustful thoughts.

_____ I am committed to doing whatever is necessary to rid my life of any pattern of sin that develops.

What are some changes you need to make

in your dating life and relationships with guys?

_____

_____

_____

_____

_____

_____

_____

_____

_____

_____

STEPPING OUT TOMORROW WITH CHRIST

The way we conduct ourselves in our relationships with guys is vital and will have lasting effects on our lives. Healthy dating relationships are built on respect—respect for ourselves, respect for the other person, and, most of all, respect for God's laws.

Unfortunately, many Christian teenagers, especially girls, believe that they will not be susceptible to sexual temptations in dating, so they do not set standards for themselves or prepare themselves for the temptations they will face. Sexual temptation in dating is one of the strongest temptations that Christians face, and many believers, including strong Christian leaders, have fallen in this area. It is easy to keep pushing back the line of what we think is acceptable, but when we do this we start down a road of sin and destruction.

91

Commitments made now in regard to having healthy relationships with people of the opposite sex will save you much heartache later on. Ask God what specific commitment He would have you make regarding this area, and write out that commitment below. Then write out three action steps that you can take to help you keep your commitment.

I promise:

_____

_____

_____

_____

_____

_____

Three action steps that will help me keep my promise:

1. _____

_____

_____

_____

2. _____

_____

_____

_____

3. _____

_____

_____

_____

Memory Verse: 1 Thessalonians 5:11

Optional Group Activities

A. Sometime between now and the next meeting, contact a Christian friend who is a guy and ask him what kinds of things Christian guys are looking for in the girls they date. Pick someone who will be honest and objective (preferably someone you are not in a dating relationship with). Take notes on what he says and bring them with you to discuss at the next meeting.

B. Think over the things that we have discussed in this section and develop a written list of standards for your dating life. Be specific, and be sure to consider ways that you can prevent any bad situations from happening in the first place. Bring your list to the next meeting for discussion.

Promise 4

GETTING SERIOUS ABOUT BIBLE STUDY AND PRAYER

Darin knew Bible study and prayer were important, but he was always so busy that he never seemed to have time. Every once in a while he would flip through the new study Bible his mom had gotten him and read a few verses, but that was about it. Then, right before Christmas during Darin's senior year, a college student named Jeff came to speak to his youth group.

When Darin heard Jeff speak, he knew this was the kind of Christian he wanted to be. Jeff seemed so close to God and so involved in what God was doing. He had been on several short-term mission trips, and he talked excitedly about what God was doing in his life. He was also very knowledge-able about the Bible and confident in speaking about God even though he was only three years older than Darin.

During Jeff's talk he mentioned that it wasn't until he'd made a commitment to Bible study and prayer that he really began to grow as a Christian, and it wasn't until then that his Christian life began to get exciting.

Darin went home that night and dug out some old notes on Bible study and prayer methods. He read through them and made a new commitment to spending time with God. If Jeff could do it, then he could too.

BUILDING A RELATIONSHIP WITH CHRIST

Teach me Thy way, O Lord; I will walk in Thy truth; Unite my heart to fear Thy name.
Psalms 86:11

Being a Christian is more than just doing certain things and not doing other things. It is a relationship with Christ. And the only way to build a relationship is to spend time with the other person.

We have addressed the need for Christian men and women to respect themselves and to show confidence and courage in their actions, but we must remember that any effectiveness or strength we have comes from Jesus Christ. If we are to be effective, it is absolutely imperative that we spend quality time getting to know Him better and availing ourselves of His power through Bible study and prayer. We need to habitually look to Him for direction and strength.

In this section we will concentrate on four activities that will be invaluable in helping you grow closer to Christ and gain wisdom and understanding for your life.

Those four areas are:

- Daily time alone with Christ ("Quiet Time")
- Prayer
- Bible study
- Scripture memorization

Making these four activities a natural part of your life will go far in deepening your faith in God. It will also help prepare you for dealing with situations that need additional attention and prayer.

Going One-on-One with Christ

Growing in our relationship with Christ begins with spending time with Him. Our first and driving love should be to spend time with Christ—one-on-one. This requires time alone with Him every day. Attending Bible studies, showing up for youth lock-ins, and going on mission trips are fine; however, these all must take second place to spending time alone with God.

Jesus talks about this one-on-one relationship in John 15:4–6. Read this passage and briefly describe below what Jesus says about this relationship.

_____

_____

_____

_____

_____

_____

_____

_____

_____

Jesus Himself set the example for one-on-one time with God. Mark 1:35 says, "And in the early morning, while it was still dark, He arose and went out and departed to a lonely place, and was praying there."

Think about that! Jesus, the Son of God, thought it was important to get alone with God. If He needed to spend time alone with His heavenly Father, then surely we should follow His lead.

Let's take a closer look at this time Jesus spent alone with God to learn more about how we should conduct our own one-on-one time.

• It was "in the early morning."

We can have our time alone with God at any time of the day, but in this case we see that Jesus chose the early morning. There is something especially satisfying about spending time alone with Him before the activities of the day begin. Also, when you meet with God early, your time with Him does not get pushed aside by other commitments. It is the first thing you do; it allows you to start your day off on the right foot.

- He "went out and departed."

Jesus was not praying from His comfortable bed, where it might be tempting to go back to sleep. Rather, He physically got up, dressed, and went to another place. Just movement alone helps to stimulate mind and body to wake up in order to focus on God.

- He went "to a lonely place."

A "lonely place" is not a depressing place but rather a place where there is no interruption from others. For us, this could be a separate room in our house. "Lonely" also suggests that we wouldn't want a television or radio on that could distract us.

- He "was praying there."

Jesus was focusing on God. Although we read our Bibles and meditate on Scripture during our daily time, our focus should be on God Himself in a spirit of prayer.

Establishing Your Own One-on-One Time

Consistently maintaining a daily time alone with Christ requires some planning. Establishing a certain time of day to have your quiet time, deciding how much time you will spend, and putting together a loose idea of what you will do during that time are all important to beginning a consistent quiet time.

Some people find that a morning quiet time doesn't work well for them. The important thing is to decide what time *is* the absolute best for you and to commit to meeting with God then. What time of day do you think is best for *you* to have a quiet time?

_____

_____

_____

There is no magic length of time for a quiet time to last. Your quiet time could be five minutes long or fifty minutes long. It's up to you. However, if you are just beginning, it is often best to shoot for seven to ten minutes. As you become used to this amount of time, try expanding it further.

And remember, your set amount of time is just a guide. Some days you may want to go longer. On other days, if you are crunched for time, recognize that it is better to spend just a few minutes with God than none at all. What amount of time do you think would work best for your quiet time at this point?

_____

_____

_____

The number one consideration for *where* you choose to have your one-on-one time with Christ is that it be a quiet place, free of distractions. That might be your bedroom. Or out on

100

the porch. Or even in a closet. And you don't have to have it in the same place every day—though it is helpful to have the place predetermined, so that you don't try to pray in the living room while your younger brother is watching cartoons, or from your bed as you drift off to sleep.

It is also important to plan to keep your quiet time schedule even when you are on vacation or somewhere else away from home. Where do you think you should plan to have your quiet time?

_____

_____

_____

_____

_____

_____

There are no set rules for what to do during a quiet time, but here's a list of ideas:

- Pray.
- Read the Bible.
- Meditate on Scripture.
- Sing praise songs.
- Write in a spiritual journal.
- Listen for God's leading.
- Review memory verses.

A Place to Start

The following is a good basic guideline for a schedule if you are just beginning to set up a quiet time:

1. Give God a big thanks for being God— 1 minute.
2. Read a few verses from the Bible— 3 minutes.
3. Pray through Scripture—4 minutes.
4. Pray for needs; thank God for answers— 2 minutes.

Prayer

Be anxious for nothing, but in everything by prayer and supplication with thanksgiving let your requests be made known to God. And the peace of God, which surpasses all comprehension, shall guard your hearts and your minds in Christ Jesus.

Philippians 4:6–7

Prayer is our direct line to God. Our most intimate communication with Him is through prayer, and prayer is the channel through which His power flows. Prayer is a crucial part of our Christian lives. It is a necessary part of our one-on-one time with God, and it should be our first response to every situation that we face. The time you spend in prayer can be meaningful and dynamic. The following are some important elements of prayer:

- Praise God for who He is and for what He has done.
- Thank God for His blessings.
- Turn your concerns and worries over to Him.
- Confess your sins and ask for forgiveness.
- Ask God for specific wisdom and direction and listen for His response.
- Admit frustrations and pains to God and ask for healing and wisdom.
- Intercede for others.
- Ask for specific requests.
- Align yourself with what God is doing in your life and in the world.
- Meditate on and pray through Scripture.

Take a minute and mark the items above that you feel you need to incorporate more into your prayer life.

One area may need more explanation—that of meditating and praying through Scripture. Many might not have tried this before or might be unsure how to begin.

Praying through Scripture is a way to personalize what God is saying through the passage and make it more a part of your life. The Psalms and Proverbs are especially good to use for this.

To pray through a passage, first read through the entire text slowly. Then, read the passage aloud. Substitute your name or the words *me* and *I* whenever possible. Last, thank God for what the passage says and for what it means to you. Meditating on Scripture may take a little time to get used to. But after a while this process can become a natural and rewarding part of your prayer time.

Let's go through an example.

Turn to Psalm 1. Read the six verses in this chapter, following the suggestions above. Personalize the passage by using your name, *I*, or *me* whenever appropriate. Repeat the verses slowly, allowing the words to sink into your heart. Then pray concerning these verses.

Developing your prayer life requires time and commitment. You may not always feel like praying. You may not always feel as if God is listening. However, consistency and persistence will pay off in a closer relationship with Christ.

It is sometimes helpful to keep a "prayer journal" in which you write down your requests along with specific answers and insights God gives you. This journal can serve as an encouragement to you and as a record of God's faithfulness.

Bible Study

All Scripture is inspired by God and profitable for teaching, for reproof, for correction, for training in righteousness; that the man of God may be adequate, equipped for every good work.

2 Timothy 3:16–17

Prayer is a powerful way to grow closer to God, but prayer goes hand in hand with studying the Bible. The Bible is God's love letter to us. We cannot follow Christ physically as the twelve apostles did in the first century, but we can get to know God's heart through reading His Word.

The Bible is the inspired Word of God. That means that He worked through man to give us the message He wanted us to have. In the Bible we can read of His interaction with man throughout history. We can know what Jesus thought and did during His life here on earth. And we can get a glimpse into God's plans for the future. The Bible is our best resource for getting to know who God is, what He desires, and what His plans for us are. Through the power of the Bible, our lives can literally be transformed.

Studying God's Word can be an exciting part of our lives. Through Bible study, we can find unlimited encouragement and wisdom. We can find insight into how to deal with our sin, our relationships, and our money. And as Christians, we have the assistance of the Holy Spirit to help us understand the Bible.

However, to get any of these benefits, we have to open our Bibles and apply ourselves to studying God's Word.

If you abide in My word, then you are truly disciples of Mine; and you shall know the truth, and the truth shall make you free.
John 8:31–32

Although there is no one right way to study the Bible, three simple steps can help you get started:

- *Step 1*: Carefully read through the passage and get an initial impression of what it is about.
- *Step 2*: Identify what is taking place. Who is speaking and to whom? What actions are taking place?
- *Step 3*: Ask yourself what you can learn from the passage and how your life should be affected by that.

This may sound simple, but these steps can greatly enhance your study efforts. In order for you to better understand these steps, let's work through a passage of Scripture using them. Read Isaiah 40:28–31 and write your responses to each of the steps in the spaces provided.

•*Step 1*:

_____

_____

_____

_____

• *Step 2:*

_____

_____

_____

_____

_____

•*Step 3:*

_____

_____

_____

_____

_____

Some ideas for Bible study are:

- Study through the four gospels.
- Do a study on Jesus' twelve apostles.
- Read about Paul and his relationship with Timothy and Barnabas.
- Pick an area of life that you are having trouble with and do a topical study on that area. (Examples: sexual purity, clean language, drinking, apathy, honoring parents.)

Scripture Memorization

Thy word I have treasured in my heart, That I may not sin against Thee.
Psalm 119:11

Nothing combats sin quite like having a heart saturated with God's Word. Romans 12:2

urges us not to be conformed to this world but to be transformed by the renewing of our mind. Scripture memorization is one of the most powerful tools for renewing the mind. By memorizing passages of the Bible, we are able to have the truth of God's Word available to us at any time in any place, and we are able to internalize the teachings we find there.

Unfortunately, there is no formula for memorizing Scripture without work. While some people may find it easier than others, most people memorize Scripture only through much time and practice. The following are some suggestions to help you get started:

- Associate the verse with a topic (such as love, forgiveness, sin).

- Always say the verse reference first, then the verse, then the reference again.

- Read through the verse repeatedly.

- Divide the verse into phrases where there are natural breaks. Begin by trying to say the verse reference and then the first phrase without looking.

- When you can say the reference and the first phrase without looking, slowly begin working on each additional phrase until you can say the whole verse without looking. (Be sure to compare what you are quoting with the verse to ensure accuracy.)

- Write down the verse from memory a few times to increase your recall potential.

- Within a day of memorizing the verse, ask a friend to check you on it. (Having a consistent partner really helps with memorization.)

- Frequently review all the verses you have memorized so that you will not forget them.

Try applying these ideas to your Promise Makers memory verses, and see if it helps. Remember, memorization is not easy for most people, so don't get discouraged. Each verse memorized is one more than you had memorized before. *Even if we memorize only one verse a month, if we do that for ten years, we will have memorized 120 verses!*

Teach me, O Lord, the way of Thy statutes, and I shall observe it to the end. Give me understanding, that I may observe Thy law, and keep it with all my heart. Make me walk in the path of Thy commandments, for I delight in it. Incline my heart to Thy testimonies, and not to dishonest gain. Turn away my eyes from looking at vanity, and revive me in Thy ways. Establish Thy word to Thy servant.
Psalm 119:33–38

Self-Evaluation

Rate yourself on a scale from 1 to 10 in the following areas, with 1 being the weakest and 10 being perfect. Then use the lines to write out what you could do to improve yourself in each area.

_____ Quiet Time

_____

_____

_____

_____

_____

_____

_____

_____ Prayer

_____

_____

_____

_____

_____

_____

_____ Bible Study

_____

_____

_____

_____

_____

_____

_____

_____ Scripture Memorization

_____

_____

_____

_____

_____

_____

STEPPING OUT TOMORROW WITH CHRIST

Making a commitment to continually grow closer to God through regular prayer, Bible study, and Scripture memorization will drastically change your life. This will be the basis for all your effectiveness for Christ and the source of your strength. Christians who do not make this commitment will soon begin to wither spiritually because they have disconnected themselves from the vine that supplies them with life.

If we firmly establish Bible study and prayer in our lives now as young men and women, we will be developing disciplines that will carry us through any future crisis that we may have to face. Devoting ourselves to Bible study and prayer will provide us with unbelievable opportunities to grow in Christ and to lead others to know Him.

God wants us to be men and women who are committed to knowing Him, to understanding His Word, and to applying its wisdom in our lives. What commitment can you make today to ensure that you will be one of those individuals? Write out your commitment below, and then list three action steps you can take to help support that commitment.

I promise:

_____

_____

_____

_____

_____

Three action steps that will help me keep my promise:

1. _____

_____

_____

_____

2. _____

_____

_____

_____

3. _____

_____

_____

_____

OPTIONAL GROUP ACTIVITIES

A. Team up with someone in your group and agree to keep each other accountable on your quiet times for at least one week. Tell each other when you plan to have your quiet time and then call each other every day just before that time as a reminder. If you are planning a morning quiet time, make sure you warn your parents about the telephone call.

B. Determine a time to meet together as a group to pray. Mention prayer requests and write them down. Determine to spend at least thirty minutes in prayer, so that no one will rush through the time. Consider going around the circle, giving each person a chance to pray, as well as spending time in silent prayer.

C. Choose one word that describes a characteristic of God and do a Bible study on that characteristic. For example, if you select God's strength as the characteristic to study, look up "strength" and any related words in a concordance to find verses that talk about His strength. Take notes on some insights you find and bring them with you to the next Promise Makers meeting.

Promise 5

FINANCIAL RESPONSIBILITY

Rachel was ecstatic when she got a job at her favorite department store. It was the first job she had ever had, and she was looking forward to finally having some cash flow. It was an added bonus that she would be working in the mall, one of her all-time favorite places.

Rachel enjoyed her new job and liked not having to ask her parents for money every time she wanted to buy something. As an employee, she also received a 15 percent discount on all merchandise, plus a store charge account. Another fringe benefit was being able to be one of the first to see all the latest fashions when they came in.

She had planned to put aside some of each paycheck to save for college, but it seemed her check was always already spent by the time she received it. It was so easy to charge things on her store account, and her employee discount made everything seem as if it were on sale anyway. She also ate out more often now with her friends and spent more money on recreation.

Rachel soon forgot about saving for college and just became concerned about keeping up with her bills. She stopped giving to her church, considering that out of the question in her financial situation. She never even seemed to have cash to buy gas for her car and was beginning to borrow money from her friends.

Rachel started requesting extra hours at work in order to make more money, but she still didn't seem to be able to get caught up. She knew her parents would be disappointed in her if they knew how much money she owed. Still she couldn't resist charging an expensive new swimsuit and buying a new portable CD player that was on sale.

TRYING TO SERVE TWO MASTERS

Money is perhaps the one thing in our lives that competes most with Christ for our attention. Jesus addresses this problem clearly in Matthew 6:24 when He says, "No one can serve two masters. Either he will hate the one and love the other, or he will be devoted to the one and despise the other. You cannot serve both God and Money" (NIV). That means we must make a choice: Will our desire for money and material things come first, or will we serve Christ alone?

Money has the power to enslave us. Covetousness can rob us of our freedom, contentment, and effectiveness as Christians. Before we even realize it, we can also become entrapped by financial problems through bad money management.

Having a proper view of material wealth and learning good money management skills early in life is crucial if we are to be free to serve Christ.

Money as a Root of Evil

But those who want to get rich fall into temptation and a snare and many foolish and harmful desires which plunge men into ruin and destruction. For the love of money is a root of all sorts of evil, and some by longing for it have wandered away from the faith, and pierced themselves with many a pang.
1 Timothy 6:9–10

Notice that the verse above doesn't say that money is a root of all sorts of evil. Instead, it says the *love* of money is the problem. Money is not evil in itself. It is a neutral object and is neither good nor bad. It is our attitude toward money that causes all kinds of evil.

We can see in Deuteronomy 14:24–26 that God allowed money to be used for the buying and selling of animals and crops. In fact, money is just a convenient system of exchanging material goods, so the *love* of money actually involves the love of all material goods.

Read Deuteronomy 14:24–26. What does this tell you about money?

_____

_____

_____

_____

_____

_____

_____

It is not a sin to go shopping or to use money to buy things, and it isn't a sin for us to have jobs that pay well. However, it *is* a sin to make money and material wealth too high a priority. Our focus should be on pleasing Christ.

When we put material things at too high a priority, our focus shifts to earning more money and buying more things. Moreover, we see what we want to have, and we often overcommit ourselves with debt. Our debts, in turn, make us more focused on material wealth and more willing to do whatever it takes to get increasing amounts of money. We become selfish. We begin to covet the things other people have. It is this coveting that sometimes causes people to steal and even murder to get what they want. God has some particular things to say about greed and covetousness. Read the following Scriptures and write out what we can learn from them on these subjects.

Deuteronomy 5:21

_____

_____

_____

_____

_____

Ephesians 5:5

_____

_____

_____

_____

James 4:2–3

_____

_____

_____

_____

God compares greed and covetousness with the sin of idolatry. They are serious and dangerous offenses in any degree. Two signs of covetousness are an obsession with gaining wealth quickly and an inability to be satisfied with what one has. Covetousness left unchecked grows like a cancer. If you see any signs of these things in your life, deal with them immediately by asking Christ's forgiveness and refocusing your life away from money and onto God's kingdom.

The Christian Outlook on Money

The area of material wealth is many times difficult to get a handle on because we all need some money to survive. Although it might be easier if we could all just swear off money altogether, the truth is that money is necessary to provide for the needs of ourselves and others. Money can be used for many good things.

However, sometimes it is hard to find the line between making money to provide for ourselves and becoming excessively concerned with money. Although the line may seem unclear at times, the difference comes down to whether or not we have the proper outlook on material wealth. Listed below are some verses that give insight into how God would have us view money. Read the verses and write out the insights you find.

Leviticus 25:23–24; Haggai 2:8

_____

_____

_____

_____

_____

1 Timothy 6:17

_____

_____

_____

1 Timothy 5:4–8

_____
_____
_____
_____

1 John 3:17–18

_____
_____
_____
_____

Proverbs 21:13; Luke 3:11

_____
_____
_____
_____

Philippians 4:14–19

_____
_____
_____
_____

Realizing that everything we have belongs to God does a lot toward releasing us from worry about financial matters. It also makes it easier for us to share what we have with others as God would have us do. Understanding how He wants us to use the things He has given us can relieve us from uncertainty and guilt. It's OK to enjoy the things God has given us as long as we are following His leading in the use of them and as long as we realize that they are His to give and His to take.

Let your character be free from the love of money, being content with what you have; for He Himself has said, "I will never desert you, nor will I ever forsake you."
Hebrews 13:5

Some Basics for Financial Responsibility

God doesn't want money to have any kind of control over us. However, if we don't learn to handle money responsibly, we can be entrapped by financial problems before we even realize it, especially in a society that offers easy credit. Below are some biblical principles that we can base our financial decisions on.

- Don't place your confidence in wealth (Proverbs 23:4–5; Ecclesiastes 5:10; Luke 12:16–21).
- Don't chase get-rich-quick schemes; do

honest work to earn money (Proverbs 13:11; 15:16; 2 Thessalonians 3:10–12).

- Live below your income potential (Proverbs 21:20).
- Stay away from overuse of credit (Proverbs 22:7).
- Ask God for wisdom, and listen to the counsel of others (Proverbs 15:22; James 1:5).

Each of these principles represents wisdom from God's Word that will provide you with financial freedom and an even greater ability to appreciate and enjoy the things God gives to you. Remember to always seek His wisdom in your spending. If we get ahead of God in our spending habits, we are setting ourselves up to start serving our things instead of serving Him.

Remember 1 Timothy 6:10. Christians have wandered away from the faith and pierced themselves with "many a pang" because they were longing for money. Chasing after wealth has led believers to pain and heartache that God never intended them to go through. To keep money from having a destructive effect in your life, make sure that you always put Christ first and that you follow the principles that God has laid out for us in His Word.

Do not be anxious then, saying, "What shall we eat?" or "What shall we drink?" or "With what shall we clothe ourselves?" . . . for your heavenly

Father knows that you need all these things. But seek first His kingdom and His righteousness; and all these things shall be added to you.
Matthew 6:31–33

Money Management Tips

God's instruction is clear about not allowing money to be the master of our lives. We must handle our money wisely so that it will not gain control over us. The following is a list of practical ways we can implement God's teachings into our spending habits and be a good steward of what He has given us:

- Buy with cash whenever possible.
- Pray about all major purchases.
- Ask God for guidance before you purchase anything on credit.
- Don't let salespeople or friends talk you into buying something you can't afford or don't need.
- Realize the difference between needs and wants.
- Never buy on impulse; think over each purchase carefully.
- Anticipate future needs and save for those things.
- If you are purchasing something that you will use for a long time, buy a quality item that will last even if you have to spend a little more for it.

- Don't let impatience push you into buying a poor quality or overpriced product.
- Don't buy things because they are on sale if you don't really need them.
- Budget your weekly/monthly spending.
- Be careful about buying products that will go out of style.

As you get older, your spending needs will change. Here are some spending tips to keep in mind for future financial decisions:

- Purchase things that will appreciate over time rather than those that will depreciate.
- Be careful of investment options that promise a high rate of return. Higher rates of return usually mean higher risks. Consider lower risk investments.
- Keep savings in interest-producing accounts such as certificates of deposits (CDs), mutual funds, and so on. Pick options that don't have too high a penalty for early withdrawal.
- Consider carefully what insurance you need. Analyze the cost versus the benefit of any insurance you buy.

Prioritizing Our Spending

Since everything is God's, we should be eager to use the things He has given us in the way He would have us use them. The New Testament talks a lot about giving—giving to churches, giving to the poor, giving to missionaries. There is no set amount stated that we should give. However, in the Old Testament the Jews were required to give tithes, which meant 10 percent of everything they had. This was the minimum requirement. What we give today is not dictated by our laws. What you decide to give is between you and God. The New Testament does give us a few guidelines, however.

In 2 Corinthians 8:12 we see that we are to give in proportion to what we have. That means the more we have, the more we should give. We see this principle again in Luke 12:48, where Jesus says: "From everyone who has been given much, much will be demanded; and from the one who has been entrusted with much, much more will be asked" (NIV). And we are also told in Luke 6:38 that what we receive will be based on how we give.

We are to be obedient to Christ in every area, including the area of giving. We should ask God what He would have us give and then give that amount obediently. Our offerings to Him should not be something that we give if we have something left over. We should instead give to Him first, in cheerful obedience, trusting Him to take care of our needs.

After we give to God the amount that He has impressed on us, the needs of our family should come next. First Timothy 5:8 tells us, "If anyone does not provide for his own, and especially for those of his household, he has denied the faith, and is worse than an unbeliever." Those are strong words, and they show that not providing for your family's needs is a serious offense to God.

After the basic needs such as food, clothing, shelter, and transportation are taken care of, we should look toward saving money for future needs and major purchases. It is only after all these things are cared for that we should spend money on luxuries and extra things.

Do not lay up for yourselves treasures upon earth, where moth and rust destroy, and where thieves break in and steal. But lay up for yourselves treasures in heaven, where neither moth nor rust destroys, and where thieves do not break in or steal; for where your treasure is, there will your heart be also.

Matthew 6:19–21

SELF-EVALUATION

Answer each question by circling either Yes or No.

Is having money too much a focus in my life?

Yes   No

Do I view my money as belonging to God?

Yes   No

Am I using my money wisely?

Yes   No

Am I spending more money than I should?

Yes   No

Do I involve God in my financial decisions?

Yes   No

Am I saving for future needs?

Yes   No

Do I see signs of materialism and covetousness in my life?

Yes   No

Am I a responsible and honest worker?

Yes   No

Have I prayed about how much God would have me give?

Yes   No

Am I giving that amount regularly?

Yes   No

Do I give to God first?

Yes   No

Am I a cheerful giver?

Yes   No

Do I put too much confidence in money?

Yes   No

STEPPING OUT TOMORROW WITH CHRIST

We live in a materialistic world. Most people would probably agree with the saying

"Money makes the world go round." However, God calls Christian men and women to hold a different view. Adopting Gods perspective on money will free us to serve Him and to enjoy life and our relationships with others. On the other hand, if we allow ourselves to be slaves to money, we will spend our lives constantly worrying about paying off our debts and purchasing more. We will never be satisfied.

Your fifth promise is one that will be regularly challenged—every time you open a magazine or view a commercial. We are constantly bombarded with messages that tell us we need even more things in order to be happy. But true, lasting happiness comes only through Christ.

Turning your personal finances over to His leadership and wisdom now will save you from many problems in the future. Think over the commitment God would have you make regarding this area and write it below. Also, write three action steps that you can take to help keep that commitment.

I promise:

_____

_____

_____

_____

_____

_____

Three action steps that will help me keep my promise:

1. _____

_____

_____

_____

2. _____

_____

_____

_____

3. _____

_____

_____

_____

Memory Verse: Matthew 6:24

OPTIONAL GROUP ACTIVITIES

A. Find someone in your church who seems to have his finances together, or a Christian businessman who specializes in the area of finances. Ask that person what advice he would give to someone just starting out in regard to managing money. Find out what he considers to be the three most important principles to remember concerning money management. Record his answers and bring them with you to the next Promise Makers session.

B. Take some time to consider what you would do if you suddenly found yourself in legal possession of $1 million. Think about what you would do with the money and record your answer to share at the next Promise Makers session.

Promise 6

SUBMITTING YOUR EGO TO GOD

Kristen had always been one of the most active members of her youth department. She was always involved in activity planning, and she often wound up doing a lot of the legwork herself. She was a member of the youth choir. She had been the one to organize a drama team and suggest that the entire youth department put on an Easter play every year. Kristen had thought that she was doing these things for the right reasons, but then Shannon started coming to her church.

Shannon was a lot like Kristen. She was outgoing, and she loved planning and organizing. She, too, was interested in music and drama, although she hadn't had the experience in those things that Kristen had.

At first, Kristen was happy to see Shannon getting so involved in the youth department, especially since she knew Shannon was a new Christian. But then Shannon started moving in on some of the things that Kristen had always done, and Kristen began feeling resentful.

However, it wasn't until the youth director suggested to Kristen that she should consider letting Shannon have the lead role in the upcoming Easter play that she became really angry. Kristen was convinced that it was only fair to give the part to the person who could play it the best, and, even though Shannon was OK at playing the part, Kristen knew she could play it better.

But then she began to wonder if the anger and resentment she felt might be an indication that she had been doing all the things in the youth department for the wrong reasons. But was it wrong to want the opportunity to use her talents for God? Didn't she deserve to have the part because she had put so much more time and work into being good at acting? Was it wrong to want to be rewarded for her hard work? Why should she have to step down and let someone else take her rightful place?

THE MENTALITY FOR SERVANTHOOD

Have this attitude in yourselves which was also in Christ Jesus, who, although He existed in the form of God . . . emptied Himself, taking the form of a bond-servant, and being made in the likeness of men.

Philippians 2:5–7

Is your focus on building up yourself or on building up others? Do you concentrate on what you think you deserve or on what you can do for others?

If there was anyone who deserved to be given recognition and power, it was Jesus. Yet the Bible tells us that He "emptied" Himself and became a servant for us. Now He calls us to take the part of a servant for Him. That doesn't mean that we can't be confident or that we shouldn't try to be good at whatever we do. But we should always examine ourselves and make sure we're serving God and not ourselves.

The balance between confidence and pride can sometimes be difficult to attain. God wants us to recognize our position in Him, but He also wants us to be willing to sacrifice our needs and wants for the good of others. Many believers have fallen because they allowed pride into their lives and put their confidence in themselves instead of God. Pride drives a wedge between us and God and undermines our efforts to serve Him. It is impossible to put aside ourselves and serve others as Christ would have us do if we do not give Him control over our egos.

Pride can slip into our lives without our even realizing it. In this section we will discuss God's perspective on ego and how to follow Christ's example of servanthood. However, before we go on, let's do a quick ego check.

Ego Check

Consider the following situations and circle the letter of the response closest to what you would normally do.

- The new kid at school needs to buy some Clearasil and wash his hair at the very least, and putting on a different shirt once in a while wouldn't hurt him either. Everyone at school makes fun of him. But since you said hi to him once when no one else was around, he's been trying to hang around with you. You . . .

    a. tell him to scram, you have a life.

    b. let him wash your car for you after school every once in a while, and figure he's lucky to get that.

    c. invite him to your church, but try to spend the minimum amount of time with him in public.

    d. thank God for bringing someone into your life you might be able to share Christ with and watch for chances to ask him to hang around with you and your friends.

- While you are at the mall with your friends, they decide to buy some great shoes and are pushing you to buy some too. Unfortunately, when you look at the price tag, you know you don't have the money to afford them. However, you do have the credit card that your parents gave you for emergencies. You . . .

    a. charge them, figuring you deserve

to have shoes as good as your
friends.

b. try to get out of it but wind up
buying them anyway.

c. pretend that you don't like the
shoes and then escape by hiding in
the sporting goods section.

d. tell your friends that you can't
afford them right now and that
you'll have to wait and find them
on sale sometime.

- You have been the announcer for the
youth group talent show for the last four
years. This year one of the younger kids
wants to be the announcer, and she is
pretty good. You . . .

  a. say, "No way! Everybody knows
  I'm the announcer."

  b. are diplomatic and put it to a vote,
  since there's no way she will win.

  c. let her be your silent assistant.

  d. quickly offer to be the behind-the-
  scenes refreshment gofer and let
  her do the announcing.

- Your 1982 Ford Fiesta is rusted out and
sounds like a sick dog on its last leg. You
pull into the school parking lot and park
beside a new red convertible. The
owner of the convertible is just getting
out of the car with a bunch of his
friends. He starts making fun of your car.

You . . .

    a. pop him. He doesn't have any right to make fun of you.

    b. yell back that at least you didn't have your daddy buy you a car.

    c. scowl in his general direction.

    d. smile and turn the other cheek. You know that your worth doesn't depend on the car you drive.

- You go to a youth rally and hear some guy saying that you need to "sell out" to Christ. He says that you must make Christ your "Lord and Master." He keeps using the words "bond servant," and he says that you should live for Christ and Christ alone. You . . .

    a. think, *Man, this guy is really off base. I'm not going to be a slave to anyone.*

    b. slide down in your seat and try not to think about what he is saying.

    c. think, *I'm all for serving God, but can't I do that and still fulfill my own dreams?*

    d. say a quick prayer asking God to help you live wholly for Him.

God's Perspective on Our Ego

Psalm 139:13–16 tells us that God personally had a hand in forming us inside our mothers' wombs and that He knew us before we were ever born. Since God made each of us, it is important to realize that He also was the one who created our ego.

Everyone has an ego. Our ego is the part of us that impacts our confidence in ourselves and determines how we think of ourselves, especially in regard to others. Ego is neither good nor bad in itself. However, the problem begins with our sin nature and how we allow our ego to develop and control our lives.

If you have a weak ego, you may not be willing to take the risks necessary to accomplish what God would have you accomplish. If your ego is too strong, you may treat others with contempt and even attempt things that foolishly endanger yourself or others. A healthy ego, however, is one that is under Christ's control and correctly balances Jesus' teachings on the confidence and power we have through Him with the servant attitude that He displayed throughout His life.

The following verses give insight into the attitudes God would have us display regarding our egos. Read the verses and write out beside them any insights you find.

Mark 10:42–45

_____

_____

_____

_____

Luke 17:7–10

_____

_____

_____

_____

Ephesians 2:8–10

_____

_____

_____

_____

Philippians 2:3

_____

_____

_____

_____

Philippians 4:13

_____

_____

_____

_____

Colossians 1:18–20

_____
_____
_____
_____

2 Timothy 1:7–9

_____
_____
_____
_____

James 3:13–18

_____
_____
_____
_____

God leaves no doubt that He is to have first place in our lives. We should be focused on glorifying Him in everything we do and say. What Christ wants should always come first, and we should always base our confidence on Christ and what He has done for us.

Letting Jesus Be Lord of Your Life

Lordship is not a word that is common in modern-day society. However, it is an important concept in regard to the Christian life. Lordship has to do with one person's being subjected to, or under the control of, another. A lord is an individual who has sovereign authority over another person or persons.

Christ is the Lord of our lives. He ransomed us by paying the penalty for our sins. He cares for us, and He has shown His love for us over and over again. Though human masters can be harsh and selfish, Jesus is perfect in love and in righteousness. He has our best interests in mind, and the only way that we can have a truly fulfilling life is by submitting ourselves to His authority.

Recognizing Jesus as our Lord means putting our personal desires under His control and being willing to do whatever He would have us do. Jesus was the perfect example of this. In His lifetime on earth, He sacrificed personal comfort and gain in order to do the Father's will, even to the point of death by crucifixion.

Jesus explains this kind of submission in Luke 9:23–24, where He says: "If anyone wishes to come after Me, let him deny himself, and take up his cross daily, and follow Me. For whoever wishes to save his life shall lose it, but whoever loses his life for My sake, he is the one who will save it."

Think about some of the phrases contained in that Scripture. Write down what the passage shows.

"If anyone wishes to come after me . . ."

_____

_____

_____

_____

_____

"let him deny himself . . ."

_____

_____

_____

_____

"and take up his cross daily, and follow Me."

_____

_____

_____

_____

"Whoever wishes to save his life shall lose it, but whoever loses his life for My sake, he is the one who will save it."

_____

_____

_____

As Christians, if we do not surrender ego, pride, and personal ambition to God, we will always have struggles. Whether or not we decide to surrender is the key to how successfully we will live our lives, how well we will model Christ's love to others, and whether or not we will grow as Christians.

Not surrendering these things to God can lead to many other sins. Most of the other areas discussed in this book depend on our obedience.

Combating Temptation Concerning Our Egos

God knows how fragile our egos are. He knows how easily we can get our feelings hurt, and He realizes how vulnerable we are to the temptation of pride and selfish ambition. He is familiar with every temptation that humans face, and He has promised to provide a way for us to be victorious over each of them.

Temptations that involve our egos can actually build us up if we use them as opportunities to recommit ourselves to Christ's lordship. The following are some steps to take when you are facing a temptation that deals with the ego:

- Realize that other Christians have faced the same temptation that you are now facing (1 Corinthians 10:13).
- Remind yourself that Christ is to have first place in everything (1 Peter 5:6).

- Remind yourself that we are not to think of ourselves as better than others and that we are to have a servant attitude (Romans 12:3).
- Remind yourself that Christ's glory is to be our number one focus, not our own glory (Ephesians 1:11–12).

Humble yourselves in the presence of the Lord, and He will exalt you.
James 4:10

SELF-EVALUATION

Rate yourself on a scale from 1 to 10 in the following areas, with 1 being the weakest and 10 being perfect.

_____ I have a servant's attitude when it comes to my relationships with others.

_____ I am able to turn the other cheek.

_____ I don't mind taking the background jobs and letting other people have the high-recognition positions.

_____ I am confident in my walk with Christ and am not timid.

_____ I put Christ first in my life.

_____ I do not view myself as better than other people.

_____ I pay attention to other people's needs.

_____ I am not chasing selfish ambitions.

Write out some temptations that you face in attempting to be a servant of Christ. Then write the response that you believe God would have you make in those situations.

_____

_____

_____

_____

_____

_____

_____

_____

_____

_____

_____

_____

_____

STEPPING OUT TOMORROW WITH CHRIST

Many guys and girls struggle with the idea of putting themselves under someone else's leadership. This is the very thing that keeps many people from coming to Christ in the first place. However, the irony is that it's only by submitting yourself to Christ that you will achieve true happiness and success. Through becoming His servant, you become worthy of the greatest honor and respect (Mark 9:35).

Many of the people we meet are trying to look out only for themselves. They put their own needs and wants above everything else, and they even try to make doing that sound like the right thing to do. But God calls us to "deny ourselves" and follow Him.

Submitting yourself to God will allow you to grow and mature as a Christian in ways you can't even imagine. It will bring peace that you didn't think was possible, and you will find that being a servant of Christ is the most exciting occupation in the world.

Think over the things discussed in this section and determine what promise God would have you make. Then write your commitment below and three action steps that will help you uphold your promise.

I promise:

_____

_____

_____

_____

_____

_____

Three action steps that will help me keep my promise:

1. _____

_____

2. _____

_____

_____

_____

3. _____

_____

_____

_____

Memory Verse: Luke 14:26–27

OPTIONAL GROUP ACTIVITIES

A. Look through the gospels and find five examples of times when Jesus could have exerted His authority but instead chose to be a servant. Write down these examples and bring them to discuss at the next Promise Makers meeting.

B. Think of three different ways that you can be a servant to someone else for Christ's sake. Take the opportunity this week to do each of these things, and take notes on what you do and how it works out. Bring your notes to the next meeting for discussion.

Promise 7

BUILDING INTEGRITY INTO YOUR LIFE

When Amber glanced over the final for government class, her heart began to pound. She wished she had stayed home and studied the night before. What was she going to do now? She read through the first five questions and realized that she didn't even know what the questions were about, let alone which of the multiple choices matched them. She glanced up. Everyone else had already started and didn't seem to be having any trouble.

Amber looked back at the test on her desk and started to try to guess the answer to the first question. But as she did, she noticed some letters scribbled on her desktop that seemed to correspond with each test question. Amber hesitated. She knew she could quietly go up and tell the teacher what she had found or even just put her paper over the answers and ignore them. However, she needed a good grade on this test so badly.

Amber's palms began to sweat. It wasn't as if she had written the answers there herself. Besides, obviously someone else had cheated on the test earlier that day, and that person got away with it. People cheated all the time.

She took a deep breath and started through her test, discreetly referring to the writing on her desk for the answers. It was just one test anyway. It wasn't as if she was going to make a habit of it, and one time wouldn't really matter. Would it?

INTEGRITY: A WAY OF LIFE

I know, my God, that you test the heart and are pleased with integrity.
                              1 Chronicles 29:17 (NIV)

What is it that keeps a high school student from cheating on a test? Or an employee from stealing a few things from work that no one would miss? What keeps a taxpayer from cheating on his taxes or a contractor from scrimping on materials? And what makes a government official able to refuse a bribe worth twice his or her yearly income?

Perhaps one of the biggest challenges that face our world today is the challenge of integrity—the commitment to being true to yourself and to your God by living according to a code of righteousness and justice.

It's a commitment to honesty and fairness,

to truth and moral uprightness. Throughout our lives, challenges to our integrity will present themselves on every side. Unfortunately, we don't have to go looking for ways to be dishonest. Opportunities often just fall into our laps, and we have to make split-second decisions.

Lack of integrity has been a problem throughout history. We don't have to look very long or hard to find examples of people who are known for dishonesty and corruption. However, it's men and women who have demonstrated wholehearted integrity that stand out above the crowd.

Integrity is not something that you can ask God for before you go to bed and wake up with in the morning. Integrity is something that must be developed through your daily walk with Him. God will supply you with the strength you need, but you must develop integrity through constant practice. Every moral decision you make will either build up your integrity or tear it down.

Daniel as an Example of Integrity

The event in Daniel's life that we are all probably most familiar with is the lions' den experience. But let's go back and look at an earlier incident that shows how Daniel must have developed the integrity that would carry him through every challenge he would face, including the lions' den.

Daniel came to Babylon as a prisoner of war. The land of Judah had just been conquered, and the king ordered that the best young men be brought to serve in his court. Daniel was one of those men. Consider the eligibility requirements that he had to meet in order to be selected (Daniel 1:3–4). He had to:

- be free from any defects
- be good-looking
- demonstrate intelligence in "every branch of wisdom"
- have understanding and knowledge
- have ability to serve in the king's court

Daniel must have been one of the cream of the crop according to Nebuchadnezzar's standards in order to be chosen. However, we find out by reading further that he was not just successful according to the world's standards, and he was not just another guy trying to get ahead through brains and good looks. Daniel was successful by God's standards, and he had a commitment to serving God no matter what.

Considering that Daniel's homeland had just been conquered and many of his family and friends killed, it is amazing that this young man was able to take the stand he did. God had set strict dietary standards for the Jews to follow. Going against this dietary law was direct disobedience to God. Yet, when Daniel arrived at the king's palace, his captors, of course, had made no provision for him to follow these special laws.

Daniel really would have had it made for the next three years. He was to learn from the smartest men, condition with the best athletes, eat the finest foods, and drink the finest wines. But Daniel refused to forget God's laws, and he "made up his mind that he would not defile himself with the king's choice food or with the wine which he drank" (Daniel 1:8).

So what happened? Read Daniel 1:1–21 to find out, and then write in your own words what Daniel did.

_____

_____

_____

_____

_____

_____

_____

_____

Daniel's choice of diet was not in itself what built integrity into his life. It was his commitment not to compromise God's standards that put him one step forward in developing a life of integrity. Daniel "made up his mind," and then he took specific actions to follow through with his commitment to please God rather than men.

Let's take a closer look at some of the things Daniel did to act in the way of integrity:

- He recognized what God would have him do and made a firm commitment to follow Him (1:8).

- He prayed regularly and faithfully (6:10).

- He made his commitment known and developed another course of action (1:8,11–13).

- He trusted God and held firmly to the course of action he had set (1:14–16).

- He gave glory to God at every opportunity (2:19, 26–28).

- He didn't forget those who had supported him (2:49).

Characteristics of Integrity

It is impossible to list all the ways that integrity can demonstrate itself in a person's life. However, the following is a list of common ways. Read through this list and mark the items that you believe you need to work on.

- Fulfillment of promises, commitments, and appointments
- Commitment to telling the truth even when it is not convenient or to your advantage
- Commitment to fairness and justice for others
- Refusal to contemplate committing wrong actions

- Strong sense of basing actions on God's instruction and will

Building integrity into your life is a lifelong process. Each item listed above represents one area in which integrity manifests itself. However, integrity is a discipline that will affect every area of your life.

How to Be a Man or Woman of Integrity

No secret formula exists for making integrity a part of our lives. Perhaps that is why it's sometimes difficult to understand what integrity is and how to incorporate it into our daily activities.

We have looked at some definitions and some examples of integrity. Now let's take a look at two key passages that give further insight into the standards God would have us meet. Beside each character trait, write how that character trait could display itself in your life.

Matthew 5:3–11

poor in spirit

_____

_____

_____

mournful

_____

_____

_____

gentle

_____

_____

_____

thirsty for righteousness

_____

_____

_____

merciful

_____

_____

_____

pure in heart

_____

_____

_____

peacemaker

_____

_____

_____

willing to be persecuted for righteousness

_____

_____

_____

Ephesians 4:25–32

be truthful

_____

_____

_____

don't sin in your anger

_____

_____

_____

don't provide opportunities for temptation

_____

_____

_____

don't steal

_____

_____

_____

work honestly

_____

_____

_____

share with others

_____

_____

_____

build up others with your speech

_____

_____

_____

put aside bitterness, malice, and slander

_____

_____

_____

be kind and tenderhearted

_____

_____

_____

But as for me, I shall walk in my integrity;
Redeem me, and be gracious to me. My foot
stands on a level place; In the congregations I
shall bless the Lord.
Psalm 26:11–12

Opportunities to Practice Integrity

You can start building integrity in your life right now by making a decision to follow the way of righteousness in every situation with which you are faced. And each time you make a decision to walk with integrity, you are strengthening this discipline in your life.

Consider each of the following areas of your life, and think of ways that you could practice integrity in them.

In your relationship with God

_____

_____

_____

In your commitment to church or youth
group

_____

_____

_____

In your relationship with your parents

_____

_____

_____

In your relationship with your siblings

_____

_____

_____

In your relationship with your friends

_____

_____

_____

In your dating

_____

_____

In your schoolwork

_____

_____

_____

In your job

_____

_____

_____

Preparation for Practicing Integrity

Practicing integrity takes strength. Someone who hasn't eaten or slept in three days is not in any condition to win a wrestling match. In the same way, if we are going to have strength to withstand the challenges that will threaten our integrity, we need to properly nourish ourselves and keep ourselves ready. The following are some things we can do to keep ourselves prepared:

- Have the proper perspective of yourself in relation to God.
- Start each day with prayer. Anticipate the integrity battles you will face and pray about them beforehand. Ask God for strength and guidance.
- Make a daily, conscious decision to do what is right every time. Determine

ahead of time that you will not be involved in anything illegal, immoral, or unethical.

- Determine that you will get out of any tempting situation as soon as possible and that, if there is no immediate way to remove yourself physically from the situation, you will tap into God's strength through prayer.
- Read your Bible regularly to stay in touch with God's righteousness.

Regularly practicing these things can do a lot to help you win the battle of integrity before you are even faced with a challenge. Take a minute to look back over these areas and circle the ones that you need to incorporate more into your life.

For as long as life is in me, and the breath of God is in my nostrils, my lips certainly will not speak unjustly, nor will my tongue mutter deceit . . . . Till I die I will not put away my integrity from me.
Job 27:3–5

Self-Evaluation
Rate yourself on a scale from 1 to 10 in the following areas, with 1 being the weakest and 10 being perfect.

_____ I am committed to walking with integrity.

_____ I always tell the truth.

_____ I always keep my promises.

_____ I never cheat on my schoolwork.

_____ I never take anything that is not mine.

_____ I always come through on commitments I have made.

_____ I am committed to fairness even when it isn't in my favor to be.

_____ I am determined to do what is right, regardless of the consequences.

_____ I respect the law and do not do anything illegal.

Note a situation regarding integrity that you have dealt with in the past or something you are currently dealing with, and write out a response to that situation that would reflect uncompromising integrity:

_____

_____

_____

_____

_____

_____

_____

_____

STEPPING OUT TOMORROW WITH CHRIST

God is looking for young men and women who will be committed to living with integrity. We live at a time when dishonesty is commonplace and society no longer even expects most promises to be kept. People are trying to convince themselves that there is no right or wrong, and justice is often perverted. But God has given us a code of righteousness to live by.

Writing a few test answers on the palm of your hand or lying to your parents about where you were Friday night may seem like small things, but each time you choose the way of dishonesty, you are tearing down integrity in your life.

Proverbs 10:9 says, "He who walks in integrity walks securely, but he who perverts his ways will be found out." In the end, integrity not only pleases God but also protects you. Building integrity into your life will help you live a life of contentment and true success, free from guilt feelings, and it will keep you from entanglements that would hinder your service to God.

Carefully consider the promise God would have you make regarding integrity, and write it below along with three action steps that will help support your promise.

I promise:

_____

_____

_____

_____

_____

_____

Three action steps that will help me keep my promise:

1. _____

_____

_____

_____

2. _____

_____

_____

_____

3. _____

_____

_____

_____

Memory Verse: 1 Corinthians 16:13

OPTIONAL GROUP ACTIVITIES

A. Read at least one newspaper during the next week and look for examples of people who have either exhibited integrity or fallen because of lack of integrity. Bring as many examples as you can find to discuss at the next Promise Makers meeting.

B. We considered Daniel in our study. Find another Bible example of someone who exhibited integrity. Do a study of that person and write down some reflections on the integrity that person displayed in his or her life. Bring your reflections to the next meeting. Be sure to include verse references.

Promise 8

IMPACTING YOUR WORLD

Zach was excited about being able to go on the summer mission trip to inner-city Chicago. All his youth group friends were going, and it would be a chance for him to get away from home and see a new place.

However, the youth pastor kept saying that everyone who went on the trip needed to know how to share his testimony and lead someone else to Christ. And that made Zach nervous. He had never done anything like that before, and he figured he wasn't really cut out for it.

Zach went to the training sessions for the trip, though, and wrote out how he had become a Christian. He memorized the required verses along with everyone else and listened to the explanations of how to use them to lead someone to Christ, but he never really thought he would get an opportunity to use them in the real world.

But during the trip, Zach got to talking to a younger kid in a mission in downtown Chicago. The youth pastor wasn't around at the moment, and he was just talking to the kid to pass some time. And then the kid started asking questions about God and how to go to heaven.

Before Zach knew it, he was answering his questions and telling him how to trust Christ, just as he had learned. When the kid prayed to receive Christ, Zach was ecstatic. He couldn't believe that God could actually use him to bring another person to a relationship with Jesus. It made him look at the rest of the mission trip in a whole different light.

BEING FISHERS OF MEN

Being a disciple of Christ involves learning from Jesus' words and example and dedicating our lives to His teachings. The word "disciple" may conjure up images of men with beards and long robes, but we need to realize that Jesus calls each of us to be a disciple of His, beard or not. When Christ called the original twelve, He had one important job in mind for them. He told Peter and Andrew, "Follow Me, and I will make you fishers of men" (Matthew 4:19).

Jesus wants His teachings to transform our lives and give us true fulfillment, but there is no way we can just stop there. We cannot put Jesus' teachings fully into our lives without reaching out to the people around us. That was

Jesus' number one goal in His life on earth.

God never intended us to isolate ourselves from unbelievers, but instead He wants us to go into the world with Christ's message. Through Christ's power in our lives, we can have a major impact on the world we live in. If we are to be true disciples, we need to commit ourselves to ministering to the world through whatever avenues God opens up to us, and we need to equip ourselves for this great calling.

Preparing Yourself

Developing our own relationship with Christ is the most effective way to prepare ourselves for reaching out to those around us. Keeping our regular time of Bible study and prayer and continually seeking direction from God are without question the most important ways of gaining strength in our Christian walk. To be most effective in our world, we need to give over every area of life to Christ, and we should be seeking to serve Him through our attitudes and actions.

However, we should never put off reaching out to those around us until we have mastered every area of Christian living. We are all human, and the Christian life is a growing experience. No matter what stage of development we are in, there are things we can do to reach out to our world.

In fact, ministry to others is part of your growth as a Christian. You might not be ready to teach a seminary theology class yet, but you can do other things that are just as important and are compatible with your strengths and Christian maturity level. From the day we accept Christ, we should be looking for ways we can share His love and message with others.

The Power of Love

You don't have to study Jesus' life very long to recognize that one of the major motivations in His life was love. He loved both the rich and the poor, the lovely and the unlovely, and He died for everyone. Jesus displayed His love for others in everything He did, including eating with sinners, healing the lame, and teaching the multitudes about God's love and forgiveness. And He calls us all to this kind of love.

True love is unconditional and not motivated by selfish desires. We should be motivated to love others simply because Christ loves them, not because they have something they can give us in return. Love for others is more than a feeling. It is a decision to act for the good of someone else. We are called to love everyone, including our enemies and those who live in unrighteousness.

It may be difficult to love friends and family in the self-sacrificing way that we should, not to mention those who are unattractive and needy or those who have wronged us in some way. But Jesus is clear about His expectations. He tells us in John 13:34 to "love one another, even as I have loved you." And in Matthew 5:43–46 He says: "You have heard that it was said, 'You shall love your neighbor, and hate your enemy.' But I say to you, love your enemies, and pray for those who persecute you in order that you may be sons of your Father who is in heaven."

Take a few minutes to think about this verse and list some people you are having difficulty loving:

1. _____

2. _____

3. _____

No one has said that loving these people will be easy. Loving our enemies is something that does not come naturally to us, and sometimes we think our hate is justified. However, through Christ's power it *is* possible to love others as Christ loves us. And it helps to continually remind ourselves that God loves that person we are having trouble loving just as much as He loves us.

In John 13:35 Jesus says, "By this all men will know that you are My disciples, if you have love for one another." Love is our most powerful tool in reaching out to others, and it should be the distinguishing quality in our lives. As 1 Peter 4:8 says, "Above all, keep fervent in your love for one another, because love covers a multitude of sins."

Below is a list of verses that give insight into Christ's expectations for our love. Read each passage and list the insights you find.

Matthew 5:21–22

_____

_____

_____

_____

_____

Ephesians 4:32

_____

_____

_____

_____

_____

Matthew 22:35–40

_____

_____

_____

_____

_____

Philippians 2:1–2

_____

_____

_____

_____

_____

Luke 6:27–28

_____

_____

_____

_____

_____

1 John 3:11–20

_____

_____

_____

_____

1 Corinthians 13:1–13

_____

_____

_____

_____

1 John 4:7–21

_____

_____

_____

_____

From these verses we see it is obvious that
demonstrating Christ's love to others should be

one of life's highest priorities. Make a list below of some ways that you can show love. Look up Matthew 25:31–40, Luke 14:12–14, and Romans 12:20 for some ideas to get yourself started.

1. _____

_____

_____

_____

2. _____

_____

_____

_____

3. _____

_____

_____

_____

4. _____

_____

_____

_____

5. _____

_____

_____

_____

The Greatest Gift We Can Give

The greatest need that every person has is to know Jesus, whether he realizes it or not. Jesus said, "I am the way, and the truth, and the life; no one comes to the Father, but through Me" (John 14:6). He is the door to heaven and to life and to peace. Without Christ, a person's life is meaningless and without hope. The good news is that Jesus has given us the mission of telling others of His love and forgiveness. The greatest gift and the greatest demonstration of love that we can give to anyone is to tell that person about Jesus' plan to redeem us from our sins.

Jesus tells us to "go therefore and make disciples of all the nations . . ." (Matthew 28:19). Do you know what "go" means in Greek? It means "go." Jesus didn't wait for people to find Him and ask Him what His mission was. He went to where the people were and began preaching His message. We don't all have to be in a full-time ministry, but we do all need to be telling others about Christ's love.

Consider this. Christ called the original twelve disciples and revealed to them His plan to save the world. Eleven of them responded positively and committed their lives to serving Him. But that wasn't the end of it. Christ taught those eleven how to tell others about Him, which began a chain that ultimately caused *us* to hear about Christ. If those eleven disciples had kept the news to themselves, you and I wouldn't be looking forward to eternity in

175

heaven. We would never have heard about Jesus. Those other disciples are long gone. Now the responsibility rests on us, and He is counting on us to keep telling people the good news.

Going can be challenging and difficult, but it is through meeting this challenge that we begin to realize how powerful and wonderful God is. Some will respond positively to our message and some negatively. We are not promised that all those we tell about Jesus will immediately repent and give their lives to Him, but we are promised that God will be with us in our going and that He will be responsible for the results. Even if the person we talk to does not respond immediately, we have planted a seed that God may use through other circumstances to bring him or her to Christ at a later time.

Going may require personal sacrifices. We may be laughed at. We may lose our popularity or even our jobs. God may ask us to leave our homes and families and go to another country. And in some parts of the world, going may require risking our lives. But our being willing to risk ourselves in order that others may have a relationship with Jesus is part of being a disciple. Remember, it cost Jesus His life on the cross.

Take a minute to list some people God might want you to tell about His love:

1. _____

2. _____

3. _____

4. _____

Sharing Your Testimony

Jesus wants to bring all people to Him. He loves every one of us. He wants to show us a better way to live. And He wants to give us true fulfillment by helping us accomplish that for which we were created.

One of the most exciting things in life is being used of God to lead someone else to Him. Some think that only pastors and missionaries can do this, but God has given each of us this mission. Many times, telling others how they can have a relationship with Him just involves telling others what Christ has done in your own life. Many Christians call this "sharing your testimony."

There isn't any particular right way to tell other people what Christ has done for you, and you don't have to tell *everything* all in one sitting. However, it is good to sit and think about what God has done for you so that you will be prepared when the opportunity arises to tell someone else.

The following are some tips to consider when developing what you will say:

- Tell what your life was like before accepting Christ.

- Tell about the circumstances that led you to accept Christ, and tell why you decided to become a Christian.

- Tell how your life is different since trusting Him and some important things you have learned since then.

- Tell about what God is doing in your life now and why others should turn to Christ.

Some who accepted Christ when they were very young may think they don't have a very powerful testimony, but this isn't true. God can use this type of testimony just as much as He can any other. If you were saved when young, focus on what God is doing *now* in your life and on the peace and meaning that He gives you.

Think about the tips listed above, and then write out your testimony below.

MY TESTIMONY

_____

_____

_____

_____

_____

_____

_____

_____

_____

_____

_____

_____

_____

_____

_____

_____

_____

_____

_____

_____

_____

_____

_____

_____

You don't necessarily need to use the same words every time you give your testimony. Writing it out is just a way to get yourself to think about what you can say. Sometime you may be asked to talk to a group without much warning, or you might unexpectedly get an opportunity to tell a friend about Christ, so you need to be prepared.

First Peter 3:15 tells us to "always be prepared to give an answer to everyone who asks you to give the reason for the hope that you have" (NIV). Writing out your testimony is one way to prepare yourself. Another way is to familiarize yourself with verses that explain God's plan of salvation, so that, if the person is ready to accept Christ, you can show him or her how from the Bible.

Leading Someone to Christ

There is no secret formula for showing

people how to trust Christ. You just need to let them see from the Bible what He has done for them. Many different passages could be used to do this, and the passages you use may depend on the particular issues a person is dealing with.

However, certain verses particularly seem to lend themselves to explaining the need for Christ and what we must do to accept Him. The following is a brief description of one way to lead someone to Christ:

Step 1. **We have all sinned.**

> *As it is written, "There is none righteous, not even one."*
>
> Romans 3:10

> *For all have sinned and fall short of the glory of God.*
>
> Romans 3:23

Step 2. **The punishment for sin is death, but God offers us eternal life.**

> *For the wages of sin is death, but the free gift of God is eternal life in Christ Jesus our Lord.*
>
> Romans 6:23

Step 3. **Jesus gave His life to take the punishment for our sins.**

> *For God so loved the world, that He gave His only begotten Son, that whoever believes in Him should not perish, but have eternal life.*
>
> John 3:16

God demonstrates His own love toward us, in that while we were yet sinners, Christ died for us.
Romans 5:8

Step 4. **All we need to do is believe in Jesus, asking Him into our lives, to have our sins forgiven and eternal life with Him.**

If you confess with your mouth Jesus as Lord, and believe in your heart that God raised Him from the dead, you shall be saved; for with the heart man believes, resulting in righteousness, and with the mouth he confesses, resulting in salvation.
Romans 10:9–10

Discipling Others

Accepting Christ is not the end of the road—it's just the beginning. A person who has just received Christ has a new life opening up to him or her, and those people need Christians who will come along beside them and help them grow in Christ. Helping a younger Christian grow is another way to impact the world. There is no way to know the effect that the encouragement or instruction you give to another Christian might have.

Right after Jesus told His disciples to go, He instructed them to teach the new Christians how to live for Him (Matthew 28:19–20). There are believers all around you who need encouragement. Many of them may look up to you without your even realizing it. Take the initiative. Give other Christians encouragement and help in their Christian walk.

List some Christians you know who you might be able to help grow in their relationship to Christ.

1. _____

2. _____

3. _____

Standing for Christ

In addition to all the opportunities you may have in your life to help people personally, you will probably also come upon situations where you simply need to take a stand for righteousness. The stand you are called to make might be to encourage righteousness in the legislature or simply to stand up to your friends for what is right. Regardless of the situation, there are some important principles to keep in mind:

- Make sure that your actions are coated in prayer. Make sure that you don't let your own ego enter the picture, and be sure to ask God for humility and guidance. Those who do not seek God's leadership in these things can many times do more harm than good.
- Make sure you show love in all your actions. Don't become so zealous that you forget the love that Christ says should define Christians. When the Phar-

isees brought the woman who was caught in adultery to Jesus to be punished, He reminded them of their own sin and said that whoever was without sin could cast the first stone (John 8:2–11). Make sure that you are not throwing stones.

- Be bold. Trust God to give you courage and stand firm. Throughout the Old and New Testaments, we can read about men who were willing to be bold for God; many at the risk of their lives. Proverbs 28:1 says, "The wicked flee when no one is pursuing, but the righteous are bold as a lion." We can be bold in our stance when we know we are doing what God would have us do. As Romans 8:31 says, "If God is for us, who can be against us?" (NIV).

SELF-EVALUATION

Rate yourself on a scale from 1 to 10 in the following areas, with 1 being the weakest and 10 being perfect.

_____ I have committed myself to being a disciple of Christ.

_____ I am actively working to impact my world for Christ.

_____ I portray Christ through my attitudes and actions.

_____ I actively show love to others.

_____ I show love to unpopular people and people who are difficult to love.

_____ I love my enemies and do good to them.

_____ I tell other people about Christ whenever I get the opportunity.

_____ I am willing to make personal sacrifices in order to bring others to Christ.

_____ I am able to tell others what Christ has done for me and how to become a Christian.

_____ I boldly stand up for Christ in love.

What changes do you need to make in your life so that you can impact your world in a greater way?

_____

_____

_____

_____

_____

_____

_____

_____

_____

_____

_____

STEPPING OUT TOMORROW WITH CHRIST

Realizing that Christ intends for us to impact our world for Him can give purpose to our lives. Whether we are in a full-time ministry in the jungles of Africa, sharing the news of Christ's love with our co-workers in a Fortune 500 company, or talking with a neighbor across the street, we can know that we are passing on the message of love and forgiveness that we were fortunate enough to receive from those who came before us.

Through God's power, we can have an unimaginable impact on our world. Talking about Christ with one person who then tells someone else can start a chain with long-reaching effects that we can't even imagine.

We cannot be obedient to God without reaching out to the world. That was Jesus' sole mission, and we can't ignore it. The rewards we will receive for following Him in this area are great, both in this lifetime and in the life to come. What promise will you make to God today regarding your commitment to impact the world? Write it below with three action steps that you can take to support your promise.

I promise:

_____

_____

_____

_____

_____

Three action steps that will help me keep my promise:

1. _____

_____

_____

_____

2. _____

_____

_____

_____

3. _____

_____

_____

_____

Memory Verse: James 1:12

OPTIONAL GROUP ACTIVITIES

A. Choose one of the younger kids in your youth group who is the same sex as you and determine to do whatever you can to help him in his Christian walk. Call him sometime during the next week and ask him to do something fun with you. Set up a time when you can get together. Find ways to get to know him better, and keep an eye out for ways to encourage and help him.

B. Identify one person you find it difficult to be around, someone who would qualify as an "unlovely" person in your eyes. Then focus your attention on trying to love that individual. Pray for him or her. Look for opportunities to show Christ's love. Make sure you apologize if you have been unkind to him or her in the past, and make it a goal in your life to put Christ's principles of love into practice concerning this person especially.

C. Choose a friend who is not a Christian and start praying for an opportunity to talk to him or her about Christ. Make a commitment that you will do whatever you can to help create a good opportunity and that you will take advantage of any opportunity that comes. Ask someone in your Promise Makers group to pray for your friend also and to keep you accountable about your commitment.

PROMISE MAKERS JOURNAL

During the past few days I have
experienced . . .

_____

_____

_____

_____

_____

_____

_____

I have experienced victory in . . .

_____

_____

_____

_____

_____

I need God's help with . . .

_____

_____

_____

_____

_____

Daily Quiet Time

Date: _____

Scripture: _____

What is going on in this Scripture?

_____

_____

_____

_____

_____

_____

_____

_____

What questions do I have about this
Scripture?

_____

_____

_____

_____

_____

_____

_____

_____

_____

How can I apply what the Scripture is saying to my life?

_____

_____

_____

_____

_____

_____

What things do I need help with?

_____

_____

_____

_____

_____

_____

Things I prayed about today:

_____

_____

_____

_____

_____

_____

Daily Quiet Time

Date: _____

Scripture: _____

What is going on in this Scripture?

_____

_____

_____

_____

_____

_____

_____

_____

What questions do I have about this
Scripture?

_____

_____

_____

_____

_____

_____

_____

_____

How can I apply what the Scripture is saying to my life?

_____

_____

_____

_____

_____

_____

What things do I need help with?

_____

_____

_____

_____

_____

_____

Things I prayed about today:

_____

_____

_____

_____

_____

_____

Daily Quiet Time

Date: _____

Scripture: _____

What is going on in this Scripture?

_____

_____

_____

_____

_____

_____

_____

_____

What questions do I have about this Scripture?

_____

_____

_____

_____

_____

_____

_____

_____

How can I apply what the Scripture is saying to my life?

_____

_____

_____

_____

_____

_____

_____

What things do I need help with?

_____

_____

_____

_____

_____

_____

Things I prayed about today:

_____

_____

_____

_____

_____

_____

Daily Quiet Time

Date: _____

Scripture: _____

What is going on in this Scripture?

_____

_____

_____

_____

_____

_____

_____

_____

_____

What questions do I have about this
Scripture?

_____

_____

_____

_____

_____

_____

_____

_____

_____

How can I apply what the Scripture is saying to my life?

_____

_____

_____

_____

_____

_____

What things do I need help with?

_____

_____

_____

_____

_____

Things I prayed about today:

_____

_____

_____

_____

_____

_____

Daily Quiet Time

Date: _____

Scripture: _____

What is going on in this Scripture?

_____

_____

_____

_____

_____

_____

_____

_____

What questions do I have about this Scripture?

_____

_____

_____

_____

_____

_____

_____

_____

How can I apply what the Scripture is saying to my life?

_____

_____

_____

_____

_____

_____

What things do I need help with?

_____

_____

_____

_____

_____

_____

Things I prayed about today:

_____

_____

_____

_____

_____

_____

Sermon/Bible Study Notes

Date: _____

Speaker: _____

Title/Topic: _____

Scripture: _____

Notes: _____

_____

_____

_____

_____

_____

_____

_____

_____

_____

How I can apply this in my life:

_____

_____

_____

_____

_____

_____

_____

_____

_____

Sermon/Bible Study Notes

Date: _____

Speaker: _____

Title/Topic: _____

Scripture: _____

Notes: _____

_____

_____

_____

_____

_____

_____

_____

_____

How I can apply this in my life:

_____

_____

_____

_____

_____

_____

_____

_____

_____

_____

Sermon/Bible Study Notes

Date: _____

Speaker: _____

Title/Topic: _____

Scripture: _____

Notes: _____

_____

_____

_____

_____

_____

_____

_____

_____

_____

How I can apply this in my life:

_____

_____

_____

_____

_____

_____

_____

_____

_____

_____

Sermon/Bible Study Notes

Date: _____

Speaker: _____

Title/Topic:_____

Scripture: _____

Notes: _____

_____

_____

_____

_____

_____

_____

_____

_____

_____

How I can apply this in my life:

_____

_____

_____

_____

_____

_____

_____

_____

_____

_____

Sermon/Bible Study Notes

Date: _____

Speaker: _____

Title/Topic: _____

Scripture: _____

Notes: _____

_____

_____

_____

_____

_____

_____

_____

_____

_____

How I can apply this in my life:

_____

_____

_____

_____

_____

_____

_____

_____

_____

Sermon/Bible Study Notes

Date: _____

Speaker: _____

Title/Topic:_____

Scripture: _____

Notes: _____

_____

_____

_____

_____

_____

_____

_____

_____

How I can apply this in my life:

_____

_____

_____

_____

_____

_____

_____

_____

_____

Sermon/Bible Study Notes

Date: _____

Speaker: _____

Title/Topic:_____

Scripture: _____

Notes: _____

_____

_____

_____

_____

_____

_____

_____

_____

_____

How I can apply this in my life:

_____

_____

_____

_____

_____

_____

_____

_____

_____

_____

Sermon/Bible Study Notes

Date: _____

Speaker: _____

Title/Topic:_____

Scripture: _____

Notes: _____

_____

_____

_____

_____

_____

_____

_____

_____

_____

How I can apply this in my life:

_____

_____

_____

_____

_____

_____

_____

_____

_____

_____

Sermon/Bible Study Notes

Date: _____

Speaker: _____

Title/Topic: _____

Scripture: _____

Notes: _____

_____

_____

_____

_____

_____

_____

_____

_____

How I can apply this in my life:

_____

_____

_____

_____

_____

_____

_____

_____

_____

For more information about Promise Makers, contact:
Promise Makers Ministries
P.O. Box 3848
Shawnee Mission, KS 66203
(913) 831-0705